# FEARLESS
# Fundraising

## FOR NONPROFIT BOARDS

### SECOND EDITION

## BY DAVE STERNBERG

### BOARDSOURCE®
*Building Effective Nonprofit Boards*

*Library of Congress Cataloging-in-Publication Data*

Sternberg, Dave.

Fearless fundraising for nonprofit boards / Dave Sternberg. — 2nd ed.

    p. cm.

Updated ed. of: Fearless fundraising for nonprofit boards / Worth George.

ISBN 1-58686-105-0 (pbk.)

1. Fund raising.   2. Nonprofit organizations — Finance.
I. George,Worth. Fearless fundraising for nonprofit boards.   II. Title.

HV41.2.G46 2008

658.15'224 — dc22

2008012666

© 2008 BoardSource.
First printing, May 2008
ISBN 1-58686-105-0

Published by BoardSource
1828 L Street, NW, Suite 900
Washington, DC 20036

**BoardSource**
*Building Effective Nonprofit Boards*

BoardSource was established in 1988 by the Association of Governing Boards of Universities and Colleges (AGB) and Independent Sector. Prior to this, in the early 1980s, the two organizations had conducted a survey and found that although 30 percent of respondents believed they were doing a good job of board education and training, the rest of the respondents reported little, if any, activity in strengthening governance. As a result, AGB and IS proposed the creation of a new organization whose mission would be to increase the effectiveness of nonprofit boards.

With a lead grant from the Kellogg Foundation and funding from five other donors, BoardSource opened its doors in 1988 as the National Center for Nonprofit Boards with a staff of three and an operating budget of $385,000. On January 1, 2002, BoardSource took on its new name and identity. These changes were the culmination of an extensive process of understanding how we were perceived, what our audiences wanted, and how we could best meet the needs of nonprofit organizations.

Today BoardSource is the premiere voice of nonprofit governance. Its highly acclaimed products, programs, and services mobilize boards so that organizations fulfill their missions, achieve their goals, increase their impact, and extend their influence. BoardSource is a 501(c)(3) organization.

### BoardSource provides

- resources to nonprofit leaders through workshops, training, and an extensive Web site (http://www.boardsource.org)

- governance consultants who work directly with nonprofit leaders to design specialized solutions to meet an organization's needs

- the world's largest, most comprehensive selection of material on nonprofit governance, including a large selection of books and CD-ROMs

- an annual conference that brings together approximately 900 governance experts, board members, and chief executives and senior staff from around the world

For more information, please visit our Web site at http://www.boardsource.org, e-mail us at mail@boardsource.org, or call us at 800-883-6262.

# Have You Used These BoardSource Resources?

## BOOKS

*Development Committee*

*Generating Buzz: Strategic Communications for Nonprofit Boards*

*Moving Beyond Founder's Syndrome to Nonprofit Success*

*The Source: Twelve Principles of Governance That Power Exceptional Boards*

*Exceptional Board Practices: The Source in Action*

*Driving Strategic Planning: A Nonprofit Executive's Guide*

*The Nonprofit Dashboard: A Tool for Tracking Progress*

*The Nonprofit Policy Sampler, Second Edition*

*Getting the Best from Your Board: An Executive's Guide to a Successful Partnership*

*The Nonprofit Board Answer Book: A Practical Guide for Board Members and Chief Executives, Second Edition*

*Self-Assessment for Nonprofit Governing Boards*

*Understanding Nonprofit Financial Statements, Third Edition*

*Transforming Board Structure: Strategies for Committees and Task Forces*

*The Board Building Cycle: Nine Steps to Finding, Recruiting, and Engaging Nonprofit Board Members, Second Edition*

*Culture of Inquiry: Healthy Debate in the Boardroom*

*The Board Chair Handbook, Second Edition*

## THE GOVERNANCE SERIES

1. *Ten Basic Responsibilities of Nonprofit Boards*

2. *Financial Responsibilities of Nonprofit Boards*

3. *Structures and Practices of Nonprofit Boards*

4. *Fundraising Responsibilities of Nonprofit Boards*

5. *Legal Responsibilities of Nonprofit Boards*

6. *The Nonprofit Board's Role in Setting and Advancing the Mission*

7. *The Nonprofit Board's Role in Planning and Evaluation*

8. *How To Help Your Board Govern More and Manage Less*

9. *Leadership Roles in Nonprofit Governance*

## DVDs

*Meeting the Challenge: An Orientation to Nonprofit Board Service*

*Speaking of Money: A Guide to Fundraising for Nonprofit Board Members*

For an up-to-date list of publications and information about current prices, membership, and other services, please call BoardSource at 800-883-6262 or visit our Web site at http://www.boardsource.org.

# Contents

# Introduction

Nonprofit boards across the United States are discussing ways of ensuring sufficient financial resources for their organizations to function. Recognizing their fiscal responsibility, board members are critiquing fundraising plans, reviewing job descriptions, and amending budgets, all in the hope of making the organization better able to sustain itself over the long term.

Often these activities are influenced by the perception that the pool of donors is shrinking. This perception has led nonprofit organizations to streamline expenses and to become more flexible, agile, and creative than ever before — all positive outcomes. However, in too many cases it has also led to rationalizations, such as those listed below, about limits on the board's ability to raise funds for the organization.

> "The economy is in recession."

> "There have been multiple natural disasters."

> "Donors are suffering from fatigue."

All of these are common explanations that nonprofit organizations use when faced with fundraising shortfalls. However, research tells a different story.

According to *Giving USA*, the annual publication of the Giving USA Foundation (http://www.givingusa.org), philanthropic giving in the United States has grown in gross dollars yearly since 1955. In 2006, philanthropic giving totaled $295 billion, or 2.1 percent of the Gross Domestic Product. Table 1 shows the sources of philanthropic giving and distribution of funds in calendar year 2006.

As Table 1 shows, donors are far from fatigued — particularly individual donors. In fact, when you combine individual contributions with bequests, individual donors accounted for almost 85 percent of total giving in the United States in 2006.

In addition, giving by individuals has increased over time. According to Giving USA, giving by individuals rose 6.4 percent (2.9 percent adjusted for inflation) between 2004 and 2005; only half of that increase reflected giving in response to major natural disasters such as Hurricane Katrina and the Indian Ocean tsunami. Between 2005 and 2006, charitable giving by individuals rose another 4.4 percent (1.2 percent adjusted for inflation).

Donors come from all income levels; "mega-gifts" from extremely wealthy donors accounted for only 1.3 percent of total individual giving in 2006. The Giving USA Foundation reports that about 65 percent of households with annual incomes under $100,000 gave to charity in 2006, and these findings are reflected in recent Center on Philanthropy at Indiana University Panel Study research.

All of this means that fundraising opportunities are increasing, rather than shrinking, particularly with respect to individual donors. Individuals are more capable of sustaining giving over time than foundations and corporations. Corporations can experience an immediate change in their charitable giving during a weak economic period, while foundations can see a decline in their investments that results in a

## TABLE 1. REPORT OF PHILANTHROPIC GIVING FOR 2006

|  | Dollar Amount | Percent of Total |
|---|---|---|
| **Total** (in billions of inflation-adjusted dollars) | $295.02 | 100 |
| **Giving by Source** |  |  |
| Individuals | 222.89 | 75.6 |
| Bequests | 22.91 | 7.8 |
| Foundations | 36.50 | 12.4 |
| Corporations | 12.72 | 4.3 |
| **Contributions Received by Type of Organization** |  |  |
| Religion | 96.82 | 32.8 |
| Education | 40.98 | 13.9 |
| Health | 20.22 | 6.9 |
| Human Services | 29.56 | 10.0 |
| Arts / Culture | 12.51 | 4.2 |
| Public Society | 21.41 | 7.3 |
| Environment | 6.60 | 2.2 |
| International Affairs | 11.34 | 3.8 |
| Gifts to Foundations | 29.50 | 10.0 |
| Unallocated | 26.08 | 8.8 |

Source: *Giving USA 2007*, a publication of the Giving USA Foundation™ researched and written by the Center on Philanthropy at Indiana University.

Note: *Giving USA* uses the Consumer Price Index to adjust for inflation. All figures are rounded. Source for foundation giving: The Foundation Center. *Giving USA* changed its rounding procedure this year. All estimates are rounded to two places, then operations are performed. In the past, operations were performed first and the results were rounded.

decrease in their grantmaking capability. Individuals, on the other hand, tend to maintain their giving because they feel a personal connection with the organizations they support. As Table 1 shows, in 2006 religious and educational organizations received nearly 50 percent of philanthropic gifts; this is because they rely heavily on gifts from individuals who have an identified and personal connection with the organization. Most nonprofit organizations that are sustainable on a yearly basis have a solid individual giving program that provides a steady income base.

However, in spite of the potential for success that fundraising with individual donors presents, fundraising is often a nonprofit board's greatest area of weakness and the greatest source of anxiety for many of its members. Some are intimidated by the thought of asking for money; others are surprised that they are expected to participate in fundraising at all. Responses to the notion that board members are expected to raise funds come in many forms:

> "No one told me I would have to raise money."

> "Isn't that a staff responsibility?"

> "I serve on the board's public relations and governance committees;
> I can't do fundraising too."

In addition, prospective board members may decline the opportunity to serve because they are not comfortable with asking others for money or giving it themselves. According BoardSource's *Nonprofit Governance Index 2007*, only 46 percent of charities have 100 percent participation in board giving, and 33 percent of board members say they are somewhat or very uncomfortable asking for money directly.

This book addresses the concerns that many board members have about fundraising. By presenting information about the fundraising process and exercises that have been used effectively by numerous consultants and trainers, it supports the development of an active fundraising culture in which board members embrace their responsibility for the fiscal health of the organization and willingly participate in raising the funds that will ensure it.

This book covers fundraising from foundations and corporations, but its primary focus is the source of the greatest potential fundraising success: individual donors. Chapter 1 provides guidance on assessing the culture of fundraising that exists in an organization and making that culture a more positive and proactive one. Chapter 2 provides an individual development plan that allows every board member to become involved in fundraising, regardless of skill or comfort level. Chapter 3 explores donor motivations and helps board members connect with those motivations in their fundraising efforts. Chapter 4 defines board and staff roles in fundraising, defines different types of fundraising activities, and describes their implementation and expected outcomes.

The included CD-ROM, *Presenting: Fundraising*, contains a Microsoft® PowerPoint® presentation on fundraising practices that can be used at board meetings to improve fundraising skills. A description of the contents of the CD-ROM is found in Appendix 1.

Many thanks to Worth George, the author of the previous edition of *Fearless Fundraising*, as well as to Edward Schumacher and Grant Thornton LLP, authors of *Capital Campaigns* and *Planned Giving*, respectively, for their contributions to this book.

It is possible through education and training to create a comfort level and role for all board members that will result in a high level of fundraising engagement. This book's goal is to enable nonprofit boards to create cultures of encouragement and sensitivity, so that all board members are motivated to participate in fundraising without fear.

# 1.

# *Plan to Succeed*

Consider the following two scenarios:

> A national gay and lesbian rights organization has a $15 million annual budget. The budget includes a substantial amount for a new program whose viability some board members have questioned. Halfway through the year the board has met twice face-to-face and raised two-thirds of the needed annual total, and every board member has either made a contribution, participated in solicitations, or both.

> An inner-city Montessori school has purchased its own building to meet growing enrollment demand, although some board members did not approve of this move. The annual budget to sustain the physical plant and support the school's operations is $12 million. Halfway through the year the board has raised only $2 million of the needed funds. Fewer than half of the board members have made donations or participated in fundraising activities, and the few who have done so harbor resentment against those who have done nothing.

The difference lies in the cultures of the two boards. The first has a culture that encourages board members to accept fundraising as a board responsibility. The second has a culture that promotes divisiveness and discourages board members from participating actively in fundraising efforts.

Even if your board is more unified than the Montessori board described above, it may have a culture that does not fully embrace fundraising. Without a culture that emphasizes and prioritizes fundraising as a role for every board member, it is difficult to sustain board engagement in fundraising over time. However, changing your board's culture, particularly with respect to fundraising, can be challenging. The first step is to understand the nature of your board's current fundraising culture.

## ASSESS THE BOARD'S FUNDRAISING CULTURE

In *Culture of Inquiry: Healthy Debate in the Boardroom* (BoardSource, 2007), Nancy Axelrod notes that "a board's culture is made up of a combination of formal and informal rules, agreements, and traditions that have developed slowly and unconsciously over time." The questions listed below cover the 13 key elements of a fundraising culture and can help your board identify the rules, agreements, and traditions that govern its approach to fundraising. Use the in-depth comments that follow each question to inform discussion and help your board identify ways in which individuals' perceptions and the larger fundraising culture need to change.

A list of the questions without the comments is provided in Appendix 2; this list can be distributed to board members as a prompt for discussion. If board members answer "no" or "not certain" to six or more of the items on the questionnaire, then there should be serious concern about the organization's fundraising culture and its ability to sustain engagement in fundraising for the long term.

1. **Are prospective board members made aware of their fundraising responsibilities before they are elected to the board?**

   It is rare for anyone in the for-profit sector to be asked to accept a job without knowing what the job responsibilities are, and prospective board members should be treated with the same basic respect. A position as a board member entails certain responsibilities, one of which is fundraising, and these should be articulated clearly from the outset.

2. **Are fundraising responsibilities and personal giving included in the board member expectation agreement?**

   Board member responsibilities are best articulated in writing, so that both the organization and the board member have a clear statement of promises and expectations. The agreement may set specific targets for combined personal giving and solicited gifts, or it may simply make a general statement that active participation in fundraising is expected.

3. **Do all or almost all board members make a yearly personal "stretch" gift to the organization's annual fund?**

   Your board members are viewed by the community as the leaders of the organization. Their behavior sets a positive model for others to follow. However, while a board member's general giving level may be made known through various forms of acknowledgment, the exact giving amount should be known only to the board chair, the executive director, and the fundraising chair unless the board member chooses to reveal it to others.

4. **Does the board chair personally solicit board members annually to ensure appropriate board giving? Does the board chair take time to personally cultivate and steward appropriate higher level prospects and donors?**

   The board chair is viewed by the board as the "leader," and it is appropriate for the leader to reinforce the organization's standards. This does not mean that the board chair must give or raise more than anyone else on the board. It does mean that the chair must model appropriate behavior through active participation in fundraising, and that the chair must not be reluctant to talk with other board members about their own participation.

5. **Does the executive director take time to personally cultivate and steward appropriate higher level prospects and donors?**

   The chief executive can ensure that donors establish a relationship with the organization as a whole, so that a board member's departure does not mean the end of the relationship with donors whom that board member has cultivated.

6. **Does the board's fundraising committee organize the board's fundraising rather than actually doing the fundraising itself?**

If a board fundraising committee results in the rest of the board members to avoid engagement in fundraising, then this committee has missed its charge.

7. **Is the organization's mission statement clear, concise, and compelling? Can all or almost all board members recite it?**

Board members must both understand and be capable of articulating the mission if they are going to be effective advocates for the organization. Board members should receive a copy of the mission statement when they are recruited to the board, and should be asked to review it once a year when they make their personal pledges of support to the organization.

8. **Beyond just reciting the organization's mission statement, can at least 80 percent of board members convincingly articulate the case for support of the organization?**

Every board member has a different style and will use different words, but the sheet music should be the same. This will help to ensure that the public is getting a consistent and accurate message. One effective way to promote correspondence among board members' presentations of the case statement is to discuss the case for support of the organization once a year at a board meeting.

9. **Does the director of development (or other staff person) identify appropriate cultivation and stewardship opportunities for board member participation?**

By tracking donor contacts and giving, an organization's staff provides vital support, letting board members know when and what type of cultivation or follow-up is needed with specific contributors.

10. **Have the chief executive and director of development presented a clear fundraising strategy to the board and solicited board input?**

When board members contribute to development of the organization's fundraising strategy, they have more of a sense of ownership of the fundraising process. In addition, when board members are informed about the strategy and aware of progress toward fundraising goals, they are better able to use the time they devote to fundraising activities.

11. **Do the chief executive and board chair organize meeting agendas to give clear priority to fundraising?**

One effective way to determine how much productive time is devoted to fundraising is to audit the minutes of board meetings. Such an audit can dispel misconceptions about how much time the board is actually devoting to this and other priority areas.

12. **Do the chief executive and board chair plan annually for board training opportunities in fundraising?**

One of the major reasons cited for not being more involved in fundraising is a lack of "know-how." One training session per year can transform both board members' feelings about fundraising and the board's fundraising culture.

13. **Do the chief executive, board chair, and director of development publicly acknowledge and recognize board members who are fulfilling their fundraising responsibilities?**

Reinforcing the positive is very powerful, both as a recognition for those who are fulfilling their responsibilities and as a stimulus for those who are not. The agenda for every board meeting should include recognition of board members who are meeting expectations.

Once your board has considered the elements that characterize a positive culture of fundraising and related them to its own situation, it can begin to think about ways to make its fundraising culture a more proactive one.

(The preceding questions were adapted from materials used by Loring, Sternberg & Associates.)

## ORIENT TOWARD FUNDRAISING SUCCESS

Change can be difficult for any organization, and it is particularly difficult when it entails changing the relationship that individuals have with the organization as a whole. A board that wants to develop a more positive fundraising culture needs to have three elements in place:

- Strong leadership from the board chair

- Commitment at the board level to the process and goals of change

- Willingness at the individual level to participate in change

### LEADERSHIP FROM THE BOARD CHAIR

The chair of the board provides a model for other members through active participation in fundraising activities. The chair also sets the tone for the board's fundraising culture by encouraging all board members to accept the fundraising role, setting the expectation that all will be donors themselves, guiding them into activities that match their talents and comfort levels, challenging them to try new things, and supporting the provision of training for board members who are new to the process of cultivation and solicitation.

The board chair needs to find ways to address board member giving without naming individuals directly. Table 2 shows one way of pointing to board members who are not giving and recognizing those who are without identifying anyone by name. (This table is adapted from materials developed by Loring, Sternberg & Associates.)

## TABLE 2. BOARD OF DIRECTORS GIVING RECORD — ANNUAL FUND

|  | 1990 | 1991 | 1992 | 1993 | 1994 | 1995 | 1996 |
|---|---|---|---|---|---|---|---|
| Board Member A | 1,550 | 1,200 | 1,350 | 2,600 | 1,080 | 2,600 | N/A |
| Board Member B | 1,100 | 1,000 | 1,000 | 1,000 | 100 | 350 | 1,000 |
| Board Member C | 1,000 | 1,000 | 1,000 | 1,000 | 2,500 | 1,500 | 1,000 |
| Board Member D | 1,078 | 1,395 | 1,304 | 1,101 | 782 | 360 | 1,028 |
| Board Member E | 500 | 500 | 500 | 500 | 3,500 | 500 | 250 |
| Board Member F | 47 | 23 | 90 | 250 | 500 | 500 | N/A |
| Board Member G | 125 | 200 | 250 | 278 | 250 | 250 | 330 |
| Board Member H | 1,000 | 100 | 1,000 | N/A | N/A | N/A | N/A |
| Board Member I | 100 | 0 | 100 | 250 | 500 | 500 | 500 |
| Board Member J | 150 | 150 | 500 | N/A | N/A | N/A | N/A |
| Board Member K | 350 | 300 | 848 | 500 | 500 | 2,500 | 175 |
| Board Member L | 100 | 100 | 150 | 275 | 250 | 250 | 250 |
| Board Member M | 200 | 0 | 500 | 1,000 | 0 | N/A | N/A |
| Board Member N | 75 | 300 | 25 | N/A | N/A | N/A | N/A |
| Board Member O | 0 | 100 | 0 | N/A | N/A | N/A | N/A |
| Board Member P | 100 | 0 | 0 | N/A | N/A | N/A | N/A |
| Board Member Q | 100 | 100 | 125 | 250 | N/A | N/A | N/A |
| Board Member R | 0 | 250 | 250 | 250 | 250 | 250 | N/A |
| Board Member S | N/A | N/A | N/A | 500 | 750 | 1,000 | 1,075 |
| Board Member T | N/A | N/A | N/A | N/A | 500 | 500 | 1,335 |
| Board Member U | N/A | N/A | N/A | N/A | 500 | 1,050 | 540 |
| Board Member V | N/A | N/A | N/A | N/A | N/A | 250 | 250 |
| Board Member W | N/A | N/A | N/A | N/A | N/A | 500 | 500 |
| Board Member X | N/A | N/A | N/A | N/A | N/A | N/A | 1,000 |
| Board Member Y | N/A | N/A | N/A | N/A | N/A | N/A | 800 |
| Board Member Z | N/A | N/A | N/A | N/A | N/A | N/A | 250 |
| # who did not give | 2 of 18 | 3 of 18 | 2 of 18 | 0 of 14 | 1 of 15 | 0 of 16 | 0 of 16 |
| average gift | 455 | 448 | 562 | 804 | 783 | 804 | 638 |
| average gift minus top 6 gifts | 135 | 147 | 249 | 319 | 356 | 371 | 404 |
| median gift | 150 | 250 | 500 | 500 | 500 | 500 | 520 |
| total gifts | 7,575 | 6,718 | 8,992 | 11,253 | 10,962 | 12,860 | 11,483 |

Using this form at the board meeting of a small education nonprofit (annual budget less than $250,000), the board chair quietly pointed to the overall giving patterns in recent years. By the end of the meeting he had received more than $12,000 in new pledges from board members whose giving performance had been below the norm. Using influence after exercising affluence can have a powerful effect on fundraising.

Beyond setting expectations for board member giving, the board chair needs to help all board members find ways of taking on active fundraising roles that match their talents, abilities, and levels of comfort. Some board members may truly enjoy the opportunity to articulate why the organization is important to them, while others will be more suited to less visible roles. Not every telephone call or personal contact needs to involve a direct request for money; raising awareness about the organization and informing donors about projects and plans are also important aspects of the overall fundraising process. What matters is not *how* board members participate, but *that* they participate. The fundraising checklist in the next chapter offers a wide array of fundraising-related activities that will enable every board member to participate in fundraising in meaningful and comfortable ways.

## BOARD COMMITMENT TO CHANGE

To develop a positive fundraising culture, a board needs to understand what is involved in making fundraising an institutional priority. A first step, particularly with boards whose primary response to the idea of fundraising is avoidance, is to demonstrate what has worked for other organizations.

- Invite the board chair of another nonprofit that has successfully engaged its board in fundraising to share the benefits of doing so.

- Share the fundraising results of nonprofits that are similar in size and/or mission and are more successful in fundraising, and stimulate a discussion of what they do that is different.

- Invite a consultant to educate the board about fundraising and how it works.

Even on a board that resists developing a positive fundraising culture, over time these steps can create enough curiosity about the subject to move your board into a more robust discussion.

Once discussion has begun, your board needs to look at the characteristics of a positive board fundraising culture and develop a plan for working toward them. A board with a positive fundraising culture has these attributes:

- All board members accept fundraising as a major part of their role. They understand that it is not enough to attend board meetings, read minutes, and as a result advocate for the status quo.

- The board discusses fundraising at every meeting.

- All board members make financial contributions to the organization themselves every year. They recognize that, by giving, they provide evidence of the organization's importance to them and thus set an example for other donors.

- The board recruitment strategy makes clear to potential board members that active participation in some aspect of fundraising is a duty of every board member. Nothing is more frustrating than asking someone to raise money when the person did not realize that doing so was expected.

- Board members participate in training that can help them expand their capabilities as fundraisers for the organization.

- Board members hold themselves and one another accountable for performance through annual self-assessments and discussion of accomplishments in relation to fundraising goals.

The importance of making fundraising an agenda item at every meeting, and the challenge that a board can face in doing so, are illustrated by the example of a Big Brothers Big Sisters affiliate. For years the board meetings of this agency followed the same predictable format: reading committee meeting minutes and discussing management functions. Eventually board members began to wonder why the affiliate was not growing, since fundraising was declared a priority. A careful review of the minutes from over two years of board meetings showed that in fact the board hardly ever spoke about fundraising at meetings.

Realizing that it would be hard to prioritize something that the board rarely, if ever, spoke about, the board moved to a consent agenda, which allowed it to focus its time and energy fundraising and marketing rather than reading and approving minutes. The outcome was incredible: Fundraising became the board's highest priority, and in just a year the affiliate's budget doubled in size.

If fundraising is to be a priority for your board, the organization needs to commit resources to developing board members' comfort with it. The resources need not be extensive; a typical option is a full-day or half-day workshop in which board members discuss the three aspects of fundraising (cultivation, solicitation, and stewardship) and practice interactions with potential donors. A set of role-plays, with facilitator instructions, is provided in Appendix 3.

Finally, in seeking to establish a positive fundraising culture, your board needs to be both affirming and patient. If your organization's board has not historically embraced fundraising as both a responsibility and an opportunity, changing the culture can be challenging. Steps in the right direction should be applauded, no matter how small, and a total transformation should not be expected to take place overnight.

## INDIVIDUAL WILLINGNESS TO PARTICIPATE IN CHANGE

In order for a board to bring about a change in its fundraising culture, all of its members need to participate in the process. Change can be difficult, even when the reasons for it are clear and compelling. The following three steps can facilitate the process.

First, invite all board members to express both their reasons for supporting the change and their reservations about it. This should be a frank and open discussion, or series of discussions if necessary, in which the views of each person are welcomed and respected. The board's assessment of its current culture can serve as the basis for discussion; the conversation may be facilitated by the board chair or by an external consultant. The goal of discussion should be to come to consensus on the need for change and to give board members who are not willing to participate assurance that their positions are respected, although the organization may have to move forward without them.

Second, adopt the use of a board member letter of agreement. This document, drafted and formally adopted by the board, fully outlines the duties involved in board membership, including both personal giving and fundraising. Agreement letters are helpful in defining standards of conduct and responsibility, and providing necessary information to prospective board members about what their peers will expect from them if they serve the organization. A sample agreement letter is provided in Appendix 4.

Third, each board member should commit to following the steps toward becoming a fearless fundraiser that are outlined in the next chapter.

When an organization's board creates the right atmosphere for fundraising, it can tap into the hidden potential of its members and give them previously unrecognized ways to use their collective talents and contacts. The fundraising culture in a boardroom can be energizing if it emphasizes the importance that fundraising plays in serving others.

# 2.

# *Get Ready to Fundraise*

As a board member, you need to understand many aspects of the fundraising process, including the fundraising environment, donor motivation, and the different types of fundraising campaigns. However, the most significant thing you can do is take on the fundraising challenge yourself. According to the *Nonprofit Governance Index 2007*, fundraising ranks #1 among areas of board performance needing improvement. This chapter is designed to assist you in developing your strengths as a fearless fundraiser.

## ACCEPT THE ROLE

The first step to becoming a fearless fundraiser is acknowledging that fundraising is a key part of your role as a board member. By accepting a position on the organization's board, you have taken on the responsibility of developing and using your skills to ensure the financial viability of the organization.

Accepting the role of fundraiser entails committing yourself in three ways:

1. *Commit yourself to the organization's mission.* Be able to recite or paraphrase the mission statement and to convey your excitement about it. Fundraising becomes a positive experience when you are enthusiastic about the programs and services that the funds will support.

2. *Commit yourself to being a donor.* Make a contribution that is in proportion to your financial capability, but give enough so that you will care how it is spent.

3. *Commit yourself to participating in the organization's fundraising program.* This does not necessarily mean making solicitations, but it does mean participating actively in some way. What matters is not how you participate, but that you participate.

Making these commitments will give you a firm foundation for success as a fundraiser. Your personal commitment will give you confidence in your own relationship with the organization and credibility in the eyes of others. You will be able to tell them why you support the organization and invite them to join you.

## CREATE YOUR ELEVATOR SPEECH AND YOUR CASE STATEMENT

As a board member, you need to be able to describe the group you serve to others in a way that conveys your interest and raises theirs. Having an elevator speech — a brief summary of what the organization is about — will stand you in good stead, whether you are making an active solicitation for funding or simply making conversation at a party.

## GABRIELLE'S STORY

Raising money is a bittersweet prospect. Organizations love how it lubricates their plans, but finding the right people to make the right ask at the right time is often a challenge, especially when it involves major giving and board volunteers.

Most chief executives are notorious for being reticent when it comes to making "the ask." Board members are even more so. It seems that no matter how many training sessions or role-playing exercises they go through, it just doesn't resonate for most board members until they taste success.

For example, Gabrielle is a board member of a food bank. The organization was in the throes of conducting its first-ever capital campaign for the construction of a new building and Gabrielle possessed a wealth of contacts, some of them family members, who had the capacity to make substantial gifts. So, of course, she became a valuable commodity to the campaign, at least until the chief executive realized that despite her passion for the organization (she used to say that she wanted to personally stand on the corner and feed children peanut butter and jelly sandwiches from her own kitchen), she was nearly paralyzed with fear when it came to face-to-face soliciting.

Nonetheless, the chief executive encouraged Gabrielle to call on her uncle with the caveat that, if she got stuck and couldn't ask, the chief executive would "rescue" her.

After some friendly conversation, the two got right to business at hand, discussing the project and the needs of the organization. Gabrielle spoke of her commitment to the organization and her feelings about what it means to serve on the board. It was the chief executive who ultimately asked the question, but both were convinced that they were successful because of Gabrielle's enthusiasm and exuberance. Without even knowing, she had secured a major gift the best way — by sharing a great story and making a strong case.

When the chief executive got the call that Gabrielle's uncle was making a significant commitment, he called her right away. After she screamed and cried at the news, Gabrielle surprised them both by saying, "Who else can I call?"

For example, imagine that you are riding to the bottom floor of an office building when a passenger remarks:

"I notice you have binder that says Board Member, Habitat for Humanity. Isn't that the organization that gives away houses to the poor?"

You reply:

"Many people think that, but we do not. The houses we build are offered through a mortgage to families that are carefully chosen. The family must assist in the construction and attend a homeowners training course. Habitat is really more about long-term outcomes, like taking kids out of homes with abuse and enabling them to have a safe and positive environment. The result is amazing…who knew that a house could change a family for generations. Want to see it firsthand?"

## BUILDING A CASE STATEMENT

1. Describe the organization through the eyes of a donor, not through the internal workings of the organization. What do you want an outsider to see? What is the mission of the organization that will most appeal to outsiders? How do people who work in the organization serve their mission? What are the clients like; how do the benefits they receive endorse the mission?

2. Remember that *people give money to make a change for the good*, not to support an organization. Donors have their own concerns and ego needs. The case statement should stress how the donation makes a difference because of the benefits it confers.

3. Position the donation as a personal investment. The people you are approaching are comfortable with the notion of investing their money. What they expect from these investments is a return. Explain the accruing impact a donation will have over the years and how benefits will compound over time.

4. Write out the case statement in detail, rather than just creating an outline or list. Doing this will help you be sure that you cover all of the key points you need to address. It will also give you confidence that you know what you are going to say when you are face to face with a potential donor.

Your elevator speech needs to articulate what the organization does, whom it serves, and how it differs from other nonprofits in the community. It needs to be clear and concise, so that you can finish speaking before the elevator doors open.

Before you can venture out into the community to solicit donors, in addition to your elevator speech, you also need to prepare your case statement. Where the elevator speech provides a quick summary, the case statement describes the organization, its values, and its impact in more detail so prospective donors quickly understand why they want to contribute.

To make your case you need to have good answers to these questions:

- What — What need does the organization fulfill?
- How — How is the organization meeting this need?
- Who — Who is the organization — its leadership, its record, its mission?
- Why — Why should the donor contribute?

As you work on your case statement, ask the board chair and the chief executive to provide information that you need about the organization's staff, its constituents, and its unique position in the community. The information they provide will help you develop an elevator speech that represents the organization in a clear and compelling way and distinguishes it from the many other worthy causes in your community.

You may find that it is easier to create the case statement first, and then summarize its elements into a succinct, coherent, emotionally persuasive elevator speech. Remember that it all comes down to the bottom line: What will be the return on the donor's gift?

## KATIE'S STORY

During a strategic planning process for a public education foundation, the board began to question the future of the organization. As a whole, they were very proud of their accomplishments and continued growth of annual fundraising revenue, but they wondered what their impact on public education would be if they could offer more grants. Offering more grants meant raising more money.

Katie, the incoming chair, was apprehensive about fundraising. She certainly understood its importance to the organization and supported the notion of future growth. As a donor she was committed to the mission and saw firsthand how contributions were used.

Over the course of the next year, the board further pursued its vision of growth. They focused on the issue at board meetings. The fundraising plan was revised to include more emphasis on cultivation and stewardship activities. The board crafted a case for a campaign and hired a consultant to test the waters.

During this time, Katie hosted several events in her home where fellow board members spoke about the organization. She accompanied other board members on personal calls to visit with potential donors. She worked with the consultant to assist in the identification of donor prospects. Katie even made a planned gift to the organization.

Within several months Katie realized that she enjoyed her role as an advocate for the foundation. Her passion was evident, and her focus on encouraging others to participate financially occurred without her even being aware she was doing it. She noted at an informal meeting with the past president that "I can't look at people any more without wondering how much money they could contribute!"

Katie learned that there is more to fundraising than asking for money. What was meaningful was *that she participated, not how she participated!*

## INCREASE YOUR KNOWLEDGE

Many people have become more careful about their giving in recent years as the result of news stories about some nonprofits' misuse of funds. Both potential and current donors are therefore likely to ask questions about how the organization uses its money, particularly how much goes to programs and how much goes to overhead. They may also want to know what the organization's plans are and how their money will assist with bringing those plans to fruition.

As a board member, you have fiduciary responsibility for the organization and should have some information on these matters already. However, in order to respond effectively to questions from donors, you need to be able to think about them from the perspective of an outsider. Remember that many people give money to make a change for the better, not to support an organization as such. They are focused on outcomes.

When interacting with potential donors, you can make a persuasive case for support of the organization if you adopt a similar focus.

- Be able to describe some of the results that the organization's programs have accomplished. Have a specific success story that you can tell.

- Be able to describe some ways that overhead is used to generate outcomes, such as by maintaining specific staff functions.

The organization's staff can provide information that will enable you to talk about outcomes in these ways.

## FIND YOUR COMFORT LEVEL — AND STRETCH IT

One way to increase your effectiveness as a fundraiser is to become involved in the fundraising process at your level of comfort and move yourself up incrementally. This approach is concrete and easy to follow, and it includes a wide range of activities that match personalities and willingness to participate. It eases fear and anxiety by providing a step-by-step process that will enable you to move from one level of involvement to the next as you are ready.

The approach is based on three levels of involvement: planning and building, friend raising, and solicitation. These are outlined in detail in the Fundraising Checklist in Appendix 5. The checklist expands the notion of fundraising to include many activities other than asking for donations, and asks for concrete information about which tasks you are willing to complete. Use the checklist to determine which level matches your comfort zone, and thus how you will initiate your involvement in fundraising.

### LEVEL ONE: PLANNING AND BUILDING

This level demands little personal risk. The tasks are activities that the board would accomplish as a group, such as planning, setting goals, and outlining priorities. These tasks involve stewardship of the organization's resources. It's critical to establish and fine-tune the fundraising plan and rationale for support. Only organized activity rooted in agreed-upon objectives can be effective in the long run. Participating in them will build your knowledge about fundraising as you help the organization to properly plan and execute its fundraising plans.

## SAMPLE LEVEL ONE PLANNING AND BUILDING ACTIVITIES

- **Assist** in drafting the fundraising case statement — a comprehensive justification for charitable support — and be able to explain it persuasively.

- **Decide** realistic budget allocations for the organization's fundraising program. (Be patient about how fast new income will be received, but ask questions, offer suggestions, and operate by agreed-upon procedures and assignments.)

- **Understand** the organization's financial situation and probable future funding position. (Resist quick fixes and short-range decisions. Probe until you become convinced money is wisely used and staff is accountable.)

- **Evaluate** progress by asking friendly — but searching — questions. (Are we doing what we agreed to do? If not, why not? Are we getting improved results as time goes on? What specifically? If not, why not? What reasonable changes might be explored?)

- **Join and get active** on at least one board committee and be alert for how its work can strengthen current fundraising endeavors. (Almost every aspect of the operation has some impact on development, directly or indirectly.)

See Appendix 5 for a full list.

## LEVEL TWO: FRIEND RAISING

This level demands more direct involvement with current and potential donors and focuses on the essential role of relationship building. By participating in the tasks at this level, you will learn more about donors and prospects while donors and prospects will learn more about the organization, its programs and services.

This level includes participation in cultivation activities such as special events, as well as stewardship of specific donors through in-person reporting of organizational accomplishments. It also includes active participation in awareness-building activities. These activities bring potential donors to the first stage of the relationship with the organization by making the connection between the potential donor's areas of interest and the organization's programs and services.

## SAMPLE LEVEL TWO ACTIVITIES

- **Provide** the names and addresses of donor prospects for the development mailing list. (Share pertinent information about your contacts: individual preferences, interest level, any misgivings about the cause, and their inclination to donate money.)

- **Research** phone numbers or secure exact addresses for campaign mailings.

- **Recruit** volunteers and prospective helpers and suggest ways to interest and to involve persons with whom you or your friends are acquainted.

- **Facilitate** introductions and access to individuals or groups where you have credibility and influence. Nurture prospects and donors on a regular basis.

- **Distribute** (hand deliver) invitations or promotional material to targeted markets: individuals, business, churches, temples, community groups, or clubs.

- **Find and relate** one or more human-interest stories to illustrate why gifts are needed and how they are used to provide, enhance, or expand your organization's outreach and impact.

- **Brainstorm** innovative ways to thank and to recognize donors. For instance, arrange a special "thank-a-thon" in which board members phone donors to express gratitude for their contributions, with no solicitation included in the conversation.

- **Assist** in fundraising special events, such as auctions, fairs, bazaars, open houses, tours, or tournaments. Enlist others to help in ways that they perceive are useful and fun, so they will want to do it again. Welcome newcomers; circulate and mingle to spread a friendly spirit, learn names, and discover common interests.

- **Host** — in your home or at a restaurant — a small group of volunteers or donor prospects to better acquaint them with the value of your organization's priorities: educational programs, advancement of a cause, or effective human-services delivery.

See Appendix 5 for a full list.

## LEVEL THREE: SOLICITATION

Level three focuses on asking others for contributions. These activities will require the greatest amount of flexibility and courage. They will also require the most patience and demand the most time. However, they will result in the greatest financial gain for the organization.

You can use the Fundraising Checklist on an annual basis (or more often, if you wish) to measure the development of your confidence as a fundraiser, identify new tasks that you would be willing to take on, and identify "stretch" tasks with which to challenge yourself. You can also use it in conjunction with the full board membership to look at the capabilities and performance of the board as a whole. Finally, you can share it with the organization's staff members, so that they can provide support and coordination for the tasks that you take on.

In completing the checklist, follow these three guiding principles:

- Be honest.

- Be realistic.

- Be willing to try something new.

## GET YOUR FEET WET

Even when you have involved yourself in the tasks outlined at Level Two, you may still feel anxiety or reluctance to move on to direct solicitation. To talk about money, you need to overcome some strong cultural and social prohibitions. In addition, the fears that many people cite about fundraising — that they will be rejected, that the person will think negatively of them, and that the person will regard the request as a transaction that implies a return gift to another charity — can be very powerful. You can help yourself overcome those feelings by working through the following process.

## 1. ROLE PLAY

Practice cultivation and solicitation scenarios with other board members — a sympathetic audience — until you are confident that you have mastered your elevator speech and can respond to different types of questions about the organization. Listen to your colleagues' feedback on your representation of the organization, and think about how to incorporate their suggestions.

Role-playing is an effective way to practice dealing with difficult situations and develop confidence in your ability to handle them. It is especially effective at providing practice in bringing a conversation to a close after a potential donor says no. Role playing also helps you to think about how you as a donor like to be treated, so that you can apply those insights to solicitation of others. Appendix 3 provides several role-playing exercises.

## 2. OBSERVE

Accompany a more experienced board member on solicitation visits. Start with a visit to a longtime supporter, where the positive outcome is certain and only the amount of the gift is in question. Such a positive experience will help you overcome anxiety by proving that donors do not bite and that it is possible to have a pleasant, collegial conversation that includes a request for money.

You may want to prepare a shortened version of your elevator speech for these observations, so that you can contribute your own perspective on the value of the organization and why you support it at an appropriate point.

Observing another board member can be especially useful when the potential donor says no. You will learn that the world does not end when this happens, and that a no often leaves the door open for a future yes.

### 3. TRY A GENERAL REQUEST

You can solicit support from a current or potential donor in a general way, without naming a specific dollar figure, to build your confidence further. For example, if you are the designated host for a potential donor at a special event, you might talk about the organization's plans for the coming year and then say, "I hope that you will consider supporting us next year. It would make a big difference." This gives you practice with solicitation and prepares the donor for a more specific request at a subsequent time.

As a board member who participates actively in fundraising, you can make a powerful contribution to the organization you serve. At the same time, you can offer potential donors the opportunity to make a difference in the community by joining you in supporting the organization and its work. When you regard fundraising as a chance to share your enthusiasm for the organization and the value of its mission, you will discover just how rewarding being a fearless fundraiser can be.

# 3.

# *Appreciate Your Donors*

Whatever type of campaign an organization is undertaking, donors are at the center of the fundraising process. Understanding donor motivation is therefore an essential prerequisite to a successful fundraising campaign.

## WHY DONORS GIVE

Donors are donors because at some level philanthropy is part of their value system. Whether because of their upbringing or because of their life circumstances, they believe that making charitable contributions is an important part of living responsibly in society.

Donors may think of their philanthropy in terms of "giving back" to a community that has supported them, or in terms of making an investment whose return will be improved quality of life for others. They may describe it as "making a difference" or "sharing the wealth" or "putting beliefs into action." Whatever the overt expression, however, charitable giving has its roots in the idea that giving is part of what is expected, and characteristic, of the kind of person the donor aspires to be.

Charitable giving is thus a transaction, even though the donor receives no goods or services. In exchange for giving, the donor obtains satisfaction and a feeling of self-worth — commodities that are intangible, but very powerful. Many have described this as an exchange of values.

---

### DONOR MOTIVATION

Donors give because

- they want to make a difference
- they are sharing their good fortune
- their beliefs are being expressed in a tangible way
- they want to invest in a worthy cause
- they are demonstrating their commitment
- someone they respect sent them an invitation
- others they know and trust are also contributing
- they seek an opportunity to change the status quo
- they want to associate themselves with the reputation of the organization
- they derive tax benefits by donating to a public charity

---

Of course, donors also obtain tax deductions, and some are motivated by the desire to direct their money to programs and services of their own choosing rather than let it be directed by the government. However, financial benefits are less of a motivator than many suppose. For example, a study conducted by Bank of America and the Center on Philanthropy at Indiana University (*Bank of America Study of High Net-Worth Philanthropy*, http://www.philanthropy.iupui.edu/Research/giving_fundraising _research.aspx #bankofamerica) found that more than half of high net-worth house-holds would continue giving at the same level if the tax deduction for charitable contributions were eliminated, and another 38 percent would decrease their giving only somewhat.

The power of the intangible returns associated with charitable giving should not be underestimated. It is a driving force that predisposes many individuals to give — and thus facilitates asking them to do so.

## HOW DONORS CHOOSE

An individual who is philanthropically inclined has a multitude of options for charitable giving. Most often, donors choose the organizations that they will support on the basis of one thing: a sense of connection with the organization.

The connection may stem from a number of sources:

- Life story: The organization plays a significant role in the donor's personal history or current activities. Examples include alumni support for educational institutions and member support for religious institutions.

- Personal values and ideals: The organization provides services or conducts activities that are consonant with the donor's values, and thus is regarded by the donor as representing a worthy cause. Examples include donor support for organizations that feed and house the homeless, and contributor support for public service broadcasting.

- Family and friends: The organization is connected to a need or situation in the life of a friend or family member, and giving enables the donor to feel that the need is being addressed in some way. Examples include gifts to a health research organization in honor of someone who was affected by disease, and gifts to an arts organization that is significant in the life of a friend or family member.

- Social network: The organization is supported by a number of friends and acquaintances whom the donor trusts and respects.

The key to initiating relationships with donors is finding (or establishing) the kinds of connections that result in charitable giving. This means being attentive to the potential donor's motivations, rather than focusing exclusively on the organization's own rationale for giving, so that the rewards associated with giving are evident to the donor.

## WHEN DONORS GIVE

Donors give when they are ready to do so, psychologically, emotionally, and financially. Financial readiness depends on the availability of funds, and it may be influenced by financial planning factors such as the need to make contributions before year's end or a dramatic change in financial situation.

Psychologically, donors give when they feel secure in their judgment about the recipient organization. Emotionally, they give when they feel inspired to do so. Donors' psychological and emotional readiness can be affected positively by a number of considerations:

- involvement in the organization or cause

- trust that the organization's representatives listen to them

- feelings of compassion

- confidence that contributions are used wisely and produce results

- knowledge that their gift will make a difference

- support for the mission

- desire to pay tribute to someone or repay for being helped

- encouragement to give from someone they respect and trust

- receipt of appropriate recognition

Successful fundraising takes place when a nonprofit's board and staff recognize the importance of these considerations and follow through by communicating with potential donors, providing opportunities for them to become involved and to give in ways that are meaningful to them (such as memorial gifts), and recognizing their contributions. By following through in these ways, a nonprofit's board and staff makes giving a rewarding experience both psychologically and emotionally, and thus lays the foundation for an ongoing relationship with the donor.

## WHY POTENTIAL DONORS FAIL TO GIVE

People often fail to give because they do not believe that the organization really needs or wants them to. They may develop this perception for numerous reasons:

- Solicitation did not interest, excite, or move them.

- Information was lacking about the difference their gift would make.

- The organization did not ask their opinion or include them in activities.

- A previous gift was not acknowledged.

However, people also fail to give, or to increase their giving, simply because they are not *asked* to do so. Informing people about the organization's work and its importance in the community is essential, but it is not enough. As every sales person knows, you've got to ask for the sale!

## BUILDING AND SUSTAINING DONOR RELATIONSHIPS

Fundraising is a marathon, not a sprint. It is a process of cultivation, solicitation, and stewardship that takes place over time. Board members need to recognize that the development of a strong base of individual donors requires repeated personal contact that reinforces the individual donor's importance to the organization.

### CULTIVATION

Cultivation is the process by which an organization builds relationships with individuals and foundations. Cultivation is often referred to as "friend raising" because the relationships that are developed lead to greater community visibility and more individual involvement with the organization, as well as greater success in solicitation. Cultivation has often been described as "building a relationship with a donor to determine the best time to seek a gift."

There are a variety of ways that members of a nonprofit board can participate in cultivation. A few ideas follow:

- Host events for potential donors in their homes.

- Discuss with close friends over dinner why they have chosen to make a planned gift to the organization.

- Greet donors at special events.

- Send a letter to colleagues informing them about the organization.

- Accompany the chief executive on a visit to a local foundation.

Participating in cultivation activities is an excellent way for board members who have not previously participated in the fundraising process to gain experience with donor interaction. When board members participate in cultivation activities, they send the message that the organization is important to them and worth the investment of their time. Because board members are volunteers, this message carries much more weight coming from them than it does coming from members of the nonprofit's staff.

## SOLICITATION

Solicitation is the process a nonprofit uses to ask for financial support. Soliciting contributions is a planned and strategic process that involves the six strategies outlined in the section on the annual campaign in Chapter 4: personal solicitation, special events, direct mail appeals, telephone appeals, Internet marketing, and proposals to foundations and corporations.

Board members may participate in solicitation activities in a variety of ways, including

- adding personalized notes to direct mail letters

- inviting friends and colleagues to special events

- working with the organization's staff on proposals, tailoring the text on the basis of their knowledge of the target foundation or corporation

- soliciting contributions directly themselves, either face to face or through a personal note or telephone call

## STEWARDSHIP

Stewardship is the notion that relationships with donors need to be maintained, as well as cultivated. By sending thank-you notes, recognizing donors in published materials, informing donors of how their contributions are being used, and inviting donor input on areas for growth and plans for development, an organization furthers its relationship with them and can engage them at a higher level, resulting in more and greater support over a long period of time.

Like cultivation, stewardship provides opportunities for board members who are new to the fundraising process to gain experience with donor interactions. Board members may participate in stewardship by

- sending personal thank-you notes

- calling current donors to update them on the organization's activities

- meeting with donors to request their ideas and input

Successful fundraising is a team effort both at the planning and execution stage. A nonprofit that is effective at raising money has developed a system in which board members and staff work as a team, melding the process of cultivation, solicitation, and stewardship with the six solicitation strategies. A highly functioning fundraising program makes the best use of both financial and human resources.

# 4.

# Understand the Process

If your nonprofit organization is to take advantage of opportunities in fundraising from individual donors, board members must be active participants in the process. All fundraising requires a high level of board involvement to reach its potential. Such involvement increases the breadth and depth of an organization's reach because each additional person who becomes involved contributes contacts, time, and ideas to the effort.

## ROLES OF BOARD AND STAFF

In effect, fundraising is a partnership between your organization's board and its staff. Board members rely on the staff to educate and inform their thinking, coordinate planning, and ultimately support their ability to raise money. The staff in exchange relies on board members to follow through on their commitments and to have the confidence in the staff's management of support activities.

In order for the partnership to work effectively, you as a board member need to understand the differences between your role and the roles of the organization's staff. The role of staff is best characterized as **development**. Development is the provision of support for the fundraising effort, including prospect research, database management, gift recording and processing, accounting, special events planning and oversight, coordination of fundraising efforts across entities within larger nonprofits, and donor relations. The development staff instigates fundraising via the development plan, and they play a role in getting the board involved. The staff is responsible for coordinating and managing the fundraising process, ensuring that fundraising goals and processes are aligned with the growth and strategic planning of the nonprofit as a whole, and ensuring that the board is involved.

**Fundraising** focuses specifically on raising money to support the organization's achievement of its mission. The board defines the context for fundraising by clarifying the organization's mission, supporting its stability, identifying its leadership, approving its budget, and planning for its future. The board must also be comfortable with the overall fundraising plan drafted by the development staff. If no specific development staff exists, it makes sense for the board to form a development committee that works on this task and presents it to the full board for input and approval.

Whoever is charged with creating the fundraising plan, all board members should be involved with carrying it out. To do this, board members participate in the three major elements of fundraising:

- Cultivation: Initiating and building relationships with donors

- Solicitation: Requesting financial support

- Stewardship: Maintaining relationships with donors and informing them of how their gifts are used

## EMPLOYING THE STAFF AS A RESOURCE

What is the role of staff in fundraising? Staff members have many opportunities to facilitate the development of a cadre of fearless fundraisers. Determine whether your organization's staff or board members handle the tasks below (if staff size at your organization is small, then the board is more likely to assume more responsibility). You can use these lists to initiate a discussion of the different roles in fundraising and determine whether or not your organization is arranged for optimal fundraising effectiveness.

The staff's role in fundraising is to

- help identify prospects

- initiate and generate ideas and draft policies

- keep files, records, and mailing lists

- manage the acknowledgment process

- conduct research

- prepare correspondence

- write proposals and reports

- assist volunteer leaders in cultivation and selected solicitation activities

The board's role in fundraising is to

- define the mission and plan for the future

- support organizational stability

- identify strong leadership

- support and approve adequate budgets

- participate in the fundraising process

An enlightened board and a smoothly functioning, well-led staff develop a natural synergy that provides a foundation of contacts, support materials, and implementation follow-up to support fearless fundraising. The seamless interface of board and staff in fundraising produces the following results:

- Staff members provide relevant background information and appropriate suggestions to help shape the board's fundraising policies.

- Staff and board work together to develop basic arguments that show why donors should contribute to the organization.

- Relationships with prospects are stronger.

Board members need to engage actively in these three elements of the fundraising process. Such active engagement allows the board to establish an environment in which relationships with donors are developed and maintained, resulting in meaningful contributions to the organization over time. A board that makes fundraising a priority and engages in it actively can create a long-term culture that revolutionizes a nonprofit.

## THE FUNDRAISING CONTEXT

Success in fundraising depends on an effective partnership between board members and staff, and also on understanding of the different ways there are to raise money. Often board and staff members begin to use fundraising terms such as "major gifts" or "capital campaign" without a clear understanding of what these terms mean or how the activities they describe relate to one another as components of an organization's overall fundraising plan. In order to conduct successful fundraising, nonprofit board members and staff need to understand the various types of fundraising activities, what each entails, and what impact each can have on the organization.

The metaphor of the four-legged stool (Figure 1) provides a useful basis for understanding the various types of fundraising. Each leg of a stool works in tandem with the other legs to hold the stool in position and make it able to bear weight. In the same way, many effective fundraising programs have four "legs" that work in tandem with one another: the annual fund, the major gifts program, the capital campaign, and the planned giving campaign. The four legs of the stool illustrate both the sources that a donor draws on to make each type of gift and the benefits of each type of gift to the recipient organization.

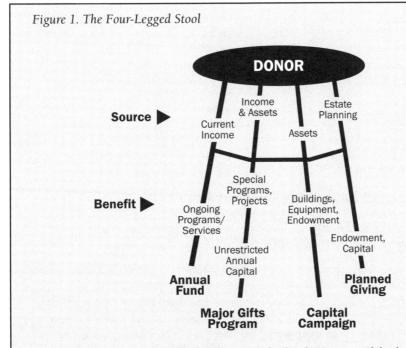

*Figure 1. The Four-Legged Stool*

Reprinted with permission from The Fund Raising School at the Center on Philanthropy at Indiana University.

The foundation of successful fundraising — the floor on which the stool rests — is a well-articulated case for support of the organization, or *case statement*. The case statement may include information on the organization's values and mission, and a statement of its value to the community. The case statement also describes the impact that a donor's gift will have on both the organization and the constituency it serves, in terms that appeal to donor interests and motivations. As a board member, you should develop your own version of the case statement, as described in Chapter 2. However, it can be helpful for board members to work together to develop a central case statement about the organization. Once you have developed the basic case for support, you can adapt it to fit the specific contexts and goals of the annual fund, major gifts program, capital campaign, and planned giving campaign.

The remainder of this chapter describes these four types of campaigns and provides guidance on how to implement them. This information is intended to allow you to determine which types are appropriate for your organization and whether you have the level of support necessary from the board and staff to initiate them.

## THE ANNUAL FUND

The annual fund typically is used to support the annual operating expenses of an organization, including program-related expenses and overhead. Gifts to the annual fund are raised through an annual campaign that results in unrestricted revenue, that is, revenue that is not designated for a specific project or use.

### PLANNING AND EXECUTING AN ANNUAL CAMPAIGN

An annual campaign involves soliciting gifts from individuals, foundations, and corporations. In planning the campaign, your organization must identify both potential donors and the solicitation strategies that will be used for each. Solicitation strategies fall into six broad categories: personal solicitation, special events, direct mail appeals, telephone appeals, Internet marketing, and proposals to foundations and corporations.

- Personal solicitation involves direct contact between the organization's board members and staff and its current or potential individual donors. Board members and staff develop and maintain personal relationships with specific individuals on the basis of mutual interest in the organization and the constituency it serves.

- Special events include both small events such as dinner parties and limited attendance receptions, and large events such as galas and golf tournaments. Many organizations use special events to introduce people to the organization and its work, as well as to thank certain donors and to solicit contributions.

- Direct mail, e-mail, and telephone appeals are generally the largest scale strategies in terms of the audience reached. These appeals draw on the organization's database of current, former, and potential donors, and may be structured in ways that encourage current donors to increase their giving or former donors to renew the relationship. These types of appeals may also be sent to smaller groups for specific purposes, such as asking a subset of donors for a second gift.

- Internet marketing involves using the organization's Web site to attract donors and enable them to give online. It also involves registering the organization with online resources such as the Network for Good (http://www.helping.org) in order to take advantage of their outreach capability.

- Proposals to foundations and corporations target benefactors whose interests are aligned with the nonprofit's mission.

By combining these strategies over a 12-month period, an annual campaign can ensure that an organization receives revenue throughout the fiscal year.

To implement an effective annual campaign, the board needs to develop a plan that sets fundraising goals for the year and outlines steps for achieving them. The goals should be based on a careful assessment of how much can be raised from whom, based on both past experience and knowledge of future prospects. The goals should also be as specific as possible.

In developing the plan for your annual campaign, include the following steps:

- Set specific goals for fundraising from individuals, foundations, and corporations.

- Identify existing and potential donors and the most effective strategies for reaching them.

- Identify untapped sources of donors and the most effective strategies for developing them.

- Develop a master calendar that outlines all fundraising-related events, including direct mail and telephone campaigns, special events, and foundation proposal deadlines.

- Assign board members and staff to each of the events on the master calendar, as appropriate.

### TAILORING THE CASE FOR SUPPORT

The case for support for the annual campaign needs to appeal to a variety of donors, many of whom will make small or modest-sized gifts. It also needs to argue convincingly that the organization's operating costs, as well as its programs, are worthy of support. The case for support thus needs to articulate the connection between the funding of annual operating expenses and the organization's ability to provide programs, so that donors see that even small gifts can have an impact on those the organization serves.

### ROLES OF BOARD MEMBERS AND STAFF

While the annual campaign is primarily a staff-driven activity, ensuring that there are enough resources to fund an organization is the board's responsibility. Successful annual campaigns require careful thought, and both board members and staff play vital roles in their planning and execution. The board and staff should work together to plan and implement fundraising efficiently so that the maximum amount of money can be raised.

In the planning stage, board members should assist in setting the fundraising goals for the year and provide input for the case for support. They may pinpoint individual donors who might be asked to increase their gifts, work with staff to identify effective strategies for reaching different types of donors, and develop untapped sources of donations (whether individual, foundation, or corporate). The staff is typically best suited to determine what the actual fundraising plan will look like. Staff can provide information about past donors, outcomes of past fundraising activities, effectiveness of various solicitation strategies, and research on prospects, and it can take the lead in developing the master calendar. The chief executive and the development staff also identify appropriate opportunities for board member participation in fundraising activities.

In the execution stage, board members may solicit contributions in person, host guests at events, host small receptions or dinners in their homes, and thank donors by phone or mail. Staff members provide coordination and logistical support for all activities. Staff members develop solicitation letters and grant proposals, design and produce direct-mail materials, conduct telephone appeals, manage special events, track donations, maintain the donor database, and produce thank-you letters for tax purposes.

The board of an environmental nonprofit had been debating a training program for its student leaders. Ed, the board chair, was especially enthusiastic about the idea, but realized that funding the program would require a major-gift effort.

As the board chair (and a large donor himself), Ed knew fundraising had to become the highest priority for the board. But it wasn't a priority, and there was no history of major-gift fundraising.

Nervous about asking for gifts of this magnitude but determined to lead by example, Ed decided to start by soliciting gifts from board members. The staff worked eagerly with Ed to quickly establish one-on-one appointments with board members about their gifts.

The chief executive knew that Ed was anxious, so she arranged for his first appointment with a close friend and long-tenured board member named Greg. Before the appointment, the chief executive informed Greg that Ed was going to meet with him over breakfast and that Greg should consider a gift of $10,000 over two years. When Ed met Greg later that week, the conversation about the campaign was brief and the gift secured.

During a board conference call the following week, Ed shared his good news about the major gift campaign.

"I have met with the first of many of you board members and the meeting was a success. Frankly, I was very anxious about 'the ask,' but Greg started our meeting by suggesting the amount that I was going to propose to him. The conversation was easy and I actually found humor in my fear," Ed reported.

Ed never knew that the chief executive had laid the framework for the meeting, but his enthusiastic explanation during the conference call energized everyone on the board. They thought, if Ed could step up and overcome his fear, so could they!

Together, board members and staff form a team with shared responsibilities and functions in the annual campaign. As paid workers, staff members carry out the detailed work that makes an annual campaign happen. As volunteers, board members connect with donors in ways that paid staff cannot. Each group thus is essential to the success of an annual campaign.

## THE MAJOR GIFTS PROGRAM

A major gifts program is a natural extension of an annual campaign because it draws on the organization's current donor base. Your organization may solicit major gifts as part of its annual campaign, in order to secure lead gifts. It may also conduct a major gifts campaign that is separate from the annual campaign, in order to raise funds for a special project or need.

The definition of a major gift depends on the nature of the other donations an organization receives, as well as the goal and budget for fundraising. A major gift to a small, start-up organization may be $500, while a large university may consider $100,000 or more to be a major gift. Major gifts may be pledged or given outright, and may come in the form of cash or appreciated assets.

It is possible to receive a major gift as the result of first-time interaction with a donor, but usually major gift opportunities will develop over time as donors gain trust in your organization, are treated in ethical and appropriate ways, and are approached with their interests in mind. Such donor development requires long-term commitment on the part of both board members and staff. Most important, a successful major gift effort relies heavily on personal contact and solicitation of donors by board members.

## PLANNING AND EXECUTING A MAJOR GIFTS PROGRAM

Because major gifts are developed over time and involve much personal interaction with donors, the first step in planning a major gifts program is ensuring that your organization is ready to acquire and manage such gifts. To determine whether your organization is ready, ask these questions:

- Is the organization as a whole committed to fundraising and to stewardship of donors and donations?

- Do the board and staff have a team approach to fundraising that involves everyone in the effort?

- Does the organization have an efficient database and staff who can manage the information and conduct prospect research to provide input to the database?

Once these readiness measures are in place, the board and staff can embark on a major gifts campaign. Major gift fundraising develops in three stages:

1. Formative: The organization is initiating relationships with potential donors, either because it is new or because it has a newly adopted fundraising orientation. At this stage, board members and staff begin to identify and build relationships with potential major gift donors. The goal is to develop donors' **interest** by making them aware of the organization's work and its contributions to the community.

2. Normative: The organization has an established donor base and an effective process for soliciting annual gifts and maintaining relationships with donors. At this stage, board members and staff invest significant time in ensuring that donors feel a sense of **involvement** with the organization. Such involvement can include making major gifts, either as lead gifts in the annual campaign or as designated gifts for specific purposes.

3. Integrative: The organization has an established and effective process for both the annual campaign and major gifts solicitation, and turns its focus to ensuring continued growth for itself and for its donors in their relationships with it. At this stage, board members and staff seek to develop donor **commitment** to making an investment that will ensure the organization's ongoing health. At this point major gifts may segue into planned giving, as donors give or pledge assets rather than cash.

## TAILORING THE CASE FOR SUPPORT

The building of a relationship that leads to major gift donations proceeds at a different pace with each individual donor. Board members and staff must therefore be willing to recognize each donor as an individual and take the time necessary to cultivate the relationship so that the donor feels connected to the organization's work and able to play a significant role in its success. With major gift donors, the case for support is a two-way street that articulates both what the donor can do for the organization and the impact the donor can have with this generosity.

Take the case of a mid-sized performing arts organization in the Midwest. In reviewing the list of season subscribers, the chief executive noticed the name of a locally prominent citizen who had been a season subscriber for over 10 years but had never made a donation. The chief executive contacted a board member, who arranged to have lunch with the subscriber just to talk about the organization's plans for the upcoming season. In the course of conversation, the subscriber described the types of performances that he enjoyed best. This opened the door for the board member to inquire whether the subscriber would be willing to support a similar performance in future. The result: a $10,000 donation to underwrite performance costs.

## ROLES OF BOARD MEMBERS AND STAFF

An efficient staff that can effectively monitor donor relationships is essential to the success of a major gifts program. Staff is responsible for tracking donors, maintaining records, and identifying annual fund donors who might be approached for major gifts. However, the heart of a major gifts program is the commitment and contributions of board members who are both willing advocates for the organization and donors to it themselves. By investing time in building and maintaining donor relationships, and especially in determining how providing a major gift will reward the donor, board members ensure the continued success of the organization's major gifts program.

# THE CAPITAL CAMPAIGN

A capital campaign is an effort over a multiyear period to raise a large amount of money for a new building, a new wing, or renovation of an existing structure. A capital campaign may raise money for equipment that will be used in the building, for the organization's operating expenses, or for an endowment to support the project long term. The project's dollar goals not only represent the specifics of the project, but can also represent a huge stretch for an organization compared to what it raises annually. In most cases, funds are sought from all available sources — individuals, corporations, national and community foundations, and governments. Usually some, if not all, of the money is raised in face-to-face solicitations. Other, typically smaller, gifts can come through direct mail, grant writing, or special events.

## PLANNING AND EXECUTING A CAPITAL CAMPAIGN

A capital campaign is highly organized, with distinct phases. A large amount of time is spent planning the campaign. For example, it is common for an organization to spend one to two years planning a five-year campaign. If your board is considering a capital campaign, keep in mind that such an arduous and long-term project may require different or additional fundraising skills than your board members now possess. Make sure you hone your board members' proficiency and comfort levels with major campaigns and engage other resourceful and skillful individuals to help on key committees.

Of the 11 steps involved in a capital campaign, the first six relate to planning and the last five to execution.

### Step 1: Define the project

Describe the project or projects to be funded and their anticipated costs in as much detail as possible. For more complex campaigns, make a list of funding priorities to define all the projects that are designated to receive funding from the campaign. The process of defining campaign priorities can be a sensitive one; you may find that campaign leaders have different priorities and must negotiate them.

### Step 2: Describe the reasons for conducting the campaign

Consider the reasons for the project and its benefits to the organization, the constituents, and the community carefully. It is the board's job to judge whether the campaign is worth the effort and whether the organization will be better off after finishing the project. When deciding whether to launch a capital campaign, board members should consider these questions:

- Will the project have a positive impact on the organization?

- Is the project necessary?

- Is the project urgent? Is it essential that the campaign be done now?

- Is the moment right to launch a capital campaign?

- Who will benefit from the project? How will it benefit the organization's constituency?

- Is the project consistent with the organization's mission and goals?

- Can the project be developed in a prudent manner with careful planning and professional advice, if necessary?

- Will the campaign strike potential donors as exciting and vital? If donors don't approve or are uninterested, the campaign could backfire.

- How will the campaign be funded? All campaigns — even those run entirely by volunteers — have expenses. How will the cost of the campaign be underwritten? Donors often want to know what percentage of the money raised will go toward the campaign.

*Step 3: Test the market*

If it is at all possible, do a feasibility study before launching the capital campaign. A feasibility or planning study is usually conducted by an outside consultant. It consists of a series of confidential interviews or focus groups with the organization's key supporters and prospective major donors to get their reaction to the project and its cost. This information is used to determine if a capital campaign has a good chance of succeeding. It may even improve the campaign's chances of success by identifying weaknesses that should be addressed before the campaign is launched and highlighting opportunities that campaign leaders may not be aware of. If the study raises serious doubts about the feasibility of a capital campaign, the board may decide to scale back, postpone, or abandon the effort.

*Step 4: Set the campaign goal*

Set a campaign fundraising goal that is as accurate as possible, because it is a benchmark by which the success of the campaign will be measured. Before setting the campaign goal, take the following issues into account:

- Determine the cost of the project. If the project is new construction, it is best to get an estimate from a contractor or builder rather than the architect, who is more likely to give a ballpark figure. Estimates on restoration and renovation work should come from someone who has experience doing such work.

- Take into account possible delays in construction and increases in costs. Thoughtful budgeting for capital projects takes into account the risk of overruns and higher prices than estimated. Most capital budgets include a contingency to cover this potential.

- Determine the cost of conducting the campaign, including staff hired for the campaign; consultants; printing, telephone, and mailing expenses; travel; special events; donor recognition; and the final celebration.

- Consider the history of fundraising in the organization. Has there been a prior campaign? How successful was it? What is the current state of fundraising? Should the project be scaled back because a previous campaign did not reach its goal or postponed in light of other current campaigns? How likely is it that major donors will give to the campaign?

- Review the results of the fundraising feasibility study. Have confidential interviews or focus groups indicated that the campaign will likely meet its goal?

The board should take steps to be sure the campaign goal is reasonable, and no campaign should start without the board's endorsement of the goal.

*Step 5: Recruit the campaign leaders*

The board chair appoints the members of the campaign steering committee. During this phase, the board and the organization's chief executive should also make a serious commitment to be involved in the campaign.

*Step 6: Develop a campaign plan*

Develop a comprehensive campaign plan based on the insight gained from the feasibility study. The plan may include a timeline, the campaign goal, campaign priorities, a list of potential contributors, and a case statement that will be shared with the public. The campaign leaders spearhead the development of the plan.

*Step 7: Identify and cultivate potential donors*

Review the list of current donors and conduct research to determine what potential donors might have an interest in the organization's work and how much they might be willing to give. Once prospects are identified, campaign leaders develop a plan to cultivate them by sending them information about the organization, giving them a tour of the facilities, or inviting them to special events. They may also ask donors to serve on committees or task forces or to act as spokespersons for the campaign. Campaign leaders also develop plans for ways of thanking donors during and after the campaign.

*Step 8: Solicit leadership gifts*

Board members and staff work together to solicit the largest gifts the organization expects to receive during the campaign. These gifts may represent as much as 80 percent of the total amount to be raised. This is sometimes called the quiet phase because it takes place before the campaign has been announced to the public. The quiet phase is often the most important stage of the campaign, because the organization concentrates its efforts on a small number of prospects with the most potential.

*Step 9: Announce the campaign to the public*

Once the leadership gifts are secured, the rest of the gifts are raised from the organization's members, donors, staff, clients, and others. This may involve direct-mail solicitations, special events, public service announcements, or other techniques. Typically the campaign is announced to the public when at least half the needed funds have been raised.

*Step 10: Recognize and thank donors*

Donors should receive a thank-you letter or card in the mail as soon as their gifts come in. Online donors may get e-mails. Some organizations offer premiums such as a mug or a book as a thank you to donors who give at a certain level. Some nonprofits list donors' names in their newsletters or on their Web sites, or hold a special event to recognize everyone who contributed. Large gifts may be recognized by plaques bearing donors' names or naming a room or building after a donor or a donor's loved one.

Recognition, both permanent and temporary, should be in place by the close of the campaign. Donors should see their names in appropriate places and on donor lists.

*Step 11: Close campaign and celebrate*

Deciding how and when to end a campaign is critical. Many organizations use one of two strategies:

- Close the campaign when the goal has been reached and a celebration can be held.

- Close the campaign when it was scheduled to close, even though it has not reached its goal. Campaign workers can then celebrate what has been raised and continue to raise more.

Regardless of the circumstances of the campaign close, the board should set out the strategy for communicating the news of the closure to the constituency, all donors, and all others involved in and affected by the campaign.

Organizations use a wide range of activities to formally close a campaign. There often is a celebration to honor the hard work and support of the campaign team, the donors, the staff, and others who were instrumental in the success of the campaign. Depending on the size of the organization and the goal of the campaign, the celebration can range from a formal reception or banquet to a casual pizza party or potluck dinner.

## TAILORING THE CASE FOR SUPPORT

Many donors are less interested in facilities themselves than in the impact those facilities will have on people. The case statement for your capital campaign thus needs to focus on people as much as or more than it focuses on bricks and mortar. It needs to convince donors that the project is solidly grounded in the values and objectives of the organization, and that its completion will increase the organization's ability to serve its constituents and contribute to the quality of life of the community. Instead of telling donors how the capital improvements will extend the life of a building, therefore, tell them how the work in the refurbished building will benefit people.

## ROLES OF BOARD MEMBERS AND STAFF

Capital campaigns are enormous undertakings that require careful planning and a serious commitment of time, energy, imagination, and patience. They engage everyone in the organization: all board members, the full staff, members of the organization when appropriate, and all the volunteers the organization can muster.

During these campaigns, the active support and endorsement of the board is essential. In fact, if the board is uncertain in any way about the viability of the effort or its value to the organization, the campaign should not move forward.

The organization's staff is instrumental in developing the project concept, obtaining architectural plans and cost estimates, and managing the logistics of the project and the capital campaign. The board operates on two levels during a capital campaign. The first is to support or endorse key decisions, and the second is to help raise money.

As decision makers, board members confirm that the project — whether new construction, renovation, equipment, or endowment — is appropriate for the organization. If so, it then authorizes the organization to conduct a campaign.

Before the campaign begins, the board authorizes the investment practices and policies that may emerge as part of the drive. Since some campaign pledges will be scheduled to come in over a period of years, the organization may get a bridge loan so construction can continue even though some of the pledges are not yet due. In addition, the board must consider the organization's policies for accepting gifts. For example, if the organization wants to offer major donors the opportunity to name a room or a building, the board must decide what level of gift earns this privilege and what, if any, limitations the organization should place on naming opportunities.

All board members are asked to "give" and "get" (to make their own donations and to help raise money from others). Each member's donation should not be a token gift but a contribution that represents a financial stretch. In addition to making their own gifts, board members are expected to help bring in donations from others. Board members also help with prospect research; for example, a board member may know that a prospect is the head of a successful business or has inherited wealth. That information can help the campaign staff determine how much to ask the donor for.

After a gift is made, board members play an active role in thanking donors. This responsibility can include sending donors thank-you notes, hosting them at recognition events, and continuing to keep them abreast of how their contributions are helping the organization and its constituents.

## MANAGING A FUNDING SHORTFALL

Even the best planned and organized campaign can fall short of its goal; perhaps the economy has taken a dip, or donors simply are not as generous as expected. This situation must be handled with care, because an organization that fails to reach its goal can suffer the consequences for years. It can face negative publicity, have trouble raising money in the future, and struggle to regain its footing.

When a funding shortfall becomes evident, your organization has several options:

- Continue with a trimmed down version of the original plan, cutting costs where possible.

- Borrow money to complete the project.

- Finish the project in phases, funding it over a longer period of time.

- Extend the length of the campaign, secure new volunteer leadership, and move forward.

- Go back to the major donors and make a case for additional funding.

You should tell leadership gift donors exactly what steps are being taken and why. You may even ask them to give again in another phase of the effort.

If the project simply cannot be built because the funding shortfall is so severe, one of three common strategies may be employed.

1. Ask donors if their gifts can be used to support another project. With major gift donors, this request should be made in person. Solicitations for smaller amounts can be made by phone or direct mail. For example, the original goal of the campaign may have been to build a new, freestanding building. The new goal might be to build a wing to an existing structure that serves part of the

same purpose. If the donors decide they want their original gift returned, do so promptly and gracefully. If donors wish you to keep the money, be sure that the use of the funds is clearly identified.

2. Offer to return the money to all donors — with the understanding that this is not always feasible because the funds have already been spent during the first phase of construction.

3. Hold the funds for a period of time, invest cautiously, and begin a new campaign in 24 to 36 months. It is wise to let donors know about the change in plans.

In any case, donors should be able to see that the organization has used their money in a thoughtful, responsible, and productive way, even if the full project is not funded. This is part of board stewardship.

## PLANNED GIVING

Planned or deferred giving is the current gift of future assets through vehicles such as bequests, charitable trusts, or annuities. The difference between a present and a deferred gift is not when the gift is made — it is when the organization can use it.

The practical reason nonprofit organizations solicit deferred gifts is that the variety of deferred giving options allows a much larger number of donors to contribute substantial amounts, especially donors who have assets but cannot afford present giving. The purpose of a planned giving program is not the immediate acquisition of funds, but the establishment of the organization's long-term financial security.

Funds generated by deferred giving programs are typically used to cover long-term expenses. Some organizations use the proceeds of deferred gifts to fund obligations that will generate income to cover long-term overhead and other types of expenses that are not usually covered by grants or other short-term sources of income. Funds obtained through planned giving may also be used to increase an organization's endowment or support special projects. The only legal restrictions on the use of the funds, once they are received, are those imposed by the donor that are contained in the trust or other legal document governing the gift.

There are a number of ways to structure a planned gift. As a board member, you do not need to know the details about structuring these plans — that function usually is performed by a staff member or a planned giving consultant — but you do need to understand their general nature, as well as information such as when the organization can expect the funds or what restrictions may be placed on a gift.

*1. Bequests*

A bequest is a gift to a beneficiary made through a will. A charitable bequest reduces the taxable estate of the donor.

Bequests generally do not require the formation of a trust or most of the other steps that make more sophisticated planned giving strategies complex. As a result, they are relatively simple for an organization to pursue and administer. Also, because bequests are relatively easy for donors to understand, they are a popular choice. Because donors making gifts do not surrender ownership of the gifted property during their lifetimes, they are often willing to make donations they otherwise would not consider.

## 2. Charitable remainder trusts

Charitable remainder trusts are the vehicles most commonly associated with deferred giving. There are three charitable remainder trust options: annuity trusts, unitrusts, and pooled income funds. The essential difference among them is how the income paid to the donor is calculated.

To create a charitable remainder trust, a donor places assets in an irrevocable trust. The trust pays income to the donor or another beneficiary, either for life or for some other stated period. The beneficiary pays taxes on that income; the trust itself is usually exempt from income taxes. At the end of the trust term, the trust assets and income pass to the charity.

When the trust is funded, the donor receives a current income tax deduction equal to the discounted present value of the charity's future interest in the trust property, actuarially determined. A charitable remainder trust can provide substantial tax advantages to the donor, especially if the donor funds the trust with appreciated assets on which the donor would otherwise pay capital gains tax. However, donors may be reluctant to relinquish control of their assets by placing them in an irrevocable trust, even when they know that they will continue to receive income.

Nonprofit organizations, too, may be uncomfortable with charitable remainder trusts. They are complicated to set up and administer; generally, a special trust agreement must be drafted. These trusts incur ongoing administrative costs to file income tax returns, invest the assets, and adhere to the terms of the trust document.

## 3. Charitable lead trusts

Charitable lead trusts are used when donors wish to provide income to a charity for a period of time, but want to either reclaim the assets or pass them on to their heirs in the future at reduced estate or gift tax valuations.

There are several different types of charitable lead trusts. Their requirements and tax consequences vary, so a nonprofit organization that wants to make this option available to its donors should ensure that it retains someone with the appropriate expertise.

## 4. Charitable gift annuities

A charitable gift annuity generates a current income tax deduction and ongoing income for the donor. However, the gift is not deferred; the recipient organization can make use of the donated cash or property immediately. Annuities are subject to state rules and regulation by state insurance departments, and they do involve administrative responsibilities. In addition, donors may be reluctant to make these gifts, because they immediately lose control of their assets.

*5. Gifts of retirement plan assets*

Many potential donors have participated in qualified retirement plans and have substantial account balances in them. These assets carry extremely high tax costs because they are subject to both estate taxes and income taxes. One way for a potential donor to mitigate some of these tax burdens is to name a nonprofit organization as the beneficiary of the plan. This eliminates both the income taxes and the estate taxes applicable to the plan.

## PLANNING AND EXECUTING A PLANNED GIVING PROGRAM

Deferred giving is a long-term proposition. While some gifts yield current benefits, in most cases organizations do not realize the value of gifts granted until some time in the future. Establishing an effective deferred giving program and gaining the first commitments can take several years; it can take even longer for the gifts to actually benefit the organization.

Careful planning is therefore vital. Before instituting a planned giving program, your board must first determine whether such a program is a good match for the organization's capabilities and culture. This means giving careful consideration to four points:

- Whether your organization has a donor base that includes likely donors, particularly donors in higher income brackets. An organization whose donor base does not include such donors will be limited in the types of planned giving that it can pursue, since donors in lower income brackets are less likely to have assets that can be placed in charitable remainder trusts.

- Whether your organization has, or can afford, the patience to allow the program to mature. Deferred giving programs often incur expenses and require volunteer and staff time for a period of time before actual revenue is realized.

- Whether your organization is willing to devote the effort and resources needed to develop the necessary specialized fundraising approach. The benefits of deferred gifts need to be explained — in person and in detail.

- Whether your organization is willing to create and maintain the staffing structure (internal staff, external professionals, or a combination of the two) needed to manage the gifts. Donations, whether received in kind or in cash, must be invested; checks must be sent to income beneficiaries at regular intervals. In addition, predicting the actual amounts that the organization will ultimately receive means understanding various factors, including actuarial statistics, inflation rates, and returns on investment.

Once your organization has determined that it is prepared to make planned giving a part of its fundraising plan, you should implement the following steps:

1. Ensure that staff supports the concept. Staff support is crucial to the success of a planned giving program; that support will evaporate quickly if board members are not committed to the program and have not made provision for obtaining needed expertise and staffing.

2. Develop materials. These include brochures and other materials, such as letters and documents, needed to present the program and the available deferred giving options. The materials should address common questions and provide the rationale for supporting the organization. They should project an image of stability, so that potential donors will see that the organization merits an investment in its future.

3. Develop a list of possible deferred giving donors. All board members and staff who know the organization's current donor base should be involved in this process; the goal is to generate a list of people who can be pursued actively. An informational mailing should also go out to the entire donor base, since some annual fund donors may have unrecognized potential as deferred gift donors.

4. Develop procedures for following up on responses to the mailing and making targeted approaches to potential donors. This will include identifying the appropriate person to make the initial contact and cultivate the relationship, as well as the right people to close the donation. The organization will also need to identify a way to answer technical questions without falling into the trap of becoming the donor's financial advisor.

5. Set up appropriate accounting procedures to handle contributions. This includes managing reporting requirements and handling the fiduciary responsibility associated with trusts.

Although it requires an up-front investment of labor and time, and involves the ongoing challenge of more complex gifts and more sophisticated fundraising strategies, when appropriate, deferred giving so greatly expands an organization's fundraising possibilities that it is well worth the effort. With careful planning and the full commitment of board members and staff, planned giving can become a key component of your organization's fundraising plan.

## TAILORING THE CASE FOR SUPPORT

Planned gifts benefit both the organization and the donor, and the key to tailoring the case for support lies in being able to make this clear to potential donors.

Donors benefit from deferred giving because they are able to make gifts without reducing their current income or undermining their financial security. Deferred gifts can augment, rather than reduce, a donor's current cash flow by reducing taxes or enabling the donor to diversify assets into those that produce income.

The benefit to the organization has to do with its long-term stability. Deferred gifts provide a source of future support that a nonprofit knows it can rely on. By making deferred gifts, donors thus make a commitment to and an investment in the future of the organization. This means that both the effect of a donor's gift and the recognition of the donor's generosity will continue for some time, particularly if the gift is structured as a trust with the donor's name on it.

## ROLES OF BOARD MEMBERS AND STAFF

The initiative for establishment of a planned giving program, and the drive to make it succeed, comes from a nonprofit organization's board. Typically, the board's development committee and the chief executive take the lead in creating the program. Board members play a crucial role in the planned giving process because they may have contacts with major donors who regard them as peers. Board members take the lead in identifying prospective donors, deciding who should contact them, and developing long-term relationships with them. Often success in obtaining a planned gift requires several visits with the donor and the donor's family, so that the board member knows how much to ask for, when to ask for it, and what reasons for giving will appeal to the donor.

Leadership from board members is the key to success in planned giving for the same reasons that it is pivotal in other types of campaigns. A planned giving program is most appropriate for certain donors:

- individuals in higher income brackets who are beginning to think about retirement

- individuals who would like to make charitable contributions but whose assets do not include much available cash

- individuals who are looking for increased return from their assets

- individuals who are holding appreciated assets

Such individuals are more likely to be peers of your organization's board members than of its staff. As a board member, you are therefore the most likely to succeed in encouraging others to participate in planned giving, especially if you have made a deferred gift yourself.

A planned giving program demands a fairly high level of management, which is the responsibility of staff. Staff members should prepare board members for visits with potential donors by conducting donor research and suggesting possible strategies, including what type(s) of planned gifts might appeal to the potential donor. Staff can also help board members by answering technical questions and helping to finalize the donation.

---

### THE POWER OF WEALTH TRANSFER

Of critical importance to the undertaking of a planned gift program is acknowledging the power of this resource. According the Center for Wealth Management at Boston College, the wealth transfer that has begun in the United States will continue until at least the year 2050. The total value of that transfer begins at $41 trillion and could be as high as $150 trillion. Clearly a nonprofit that embraces planned gifts is in a much better position to receive some of this wealth transfer.

---

However, planned giving programs are complicated undertakings that require technical skills and specialized knowledge that are often beyond the expertise of both board members and staff. In certain key areas, such as the financial administration of gift vehicles, investment of the principal of the planned gifts, life income payments, and planned giving prospect management, your organization will need to rely on one or more external professionals. Outside consultants or staff members — not board members — should handle the technical aspects of the program, including monitoring limitations on gifts and meeting regulatory guidelines. A financial advisor can explain how different types of gifts are structured, how each will affect your organization, and which plans are likely to appeal to which potential donors. The degree to which you need such external assistance will depend on the level of expertise available among your organization's staff.

# Conclusion

The late Hank Rosso, a long-time fundraising consultant and the founder of the Fund Raising School, referred to fundraising as "the gentle art of teaching the joy of giving." As this book shows, fundraising is about so much more than asking for money. It is about helping others to find ways to reach beyond themselves. When soliciting gifts, keep in mind that you are simply a conduit that connects those who want to make a difference with a tangible way of doing so.

While one could assert that there are finite resources for philanthropy, it is fair to assume that we have not yet reached that limit. Philanthropic dollars grow each year in response to the needs in our communities. Resources are available to every nonprofit that can harness its capacity to reach them.

As a board member, you are an essential part of that capacity. Your enthusiasm for the organization's mission and your commitment to supporting it will enable you to engage fearlessly in promoting, advocating for, and soliciting on behalf of the nonprofit you serve — that is, to teach the joy of giving through your own example.

The resources available are plentiful. There is no better time to start teaching!

# *Appendix 1. About the CD-ROM*

The attached CD-ROM contains the electronic form of *Presenting: Fundraising: The Board Member's Role in Resource Development*. The tools on this CD-ROM are published by BoardSource and can be used as is or, in some cases, customized for your organization's needs.

The CD-ROM contains suggestions for who should make the presentation (someone familiar with your organization's fundraising programs) and who should view the presentation (*every* board member). The CD-ROM contains a set of slides divided into four sections:

Section 1: Fundraising Responsibilities
Section 2: Fundraising Facts and Figures
Section 3: The Stages of Fundraising
Section 4: The Types of Fundraising

The files on this CD-ROM are in three formats:

- Microsoft® PowerPoint® graphics presentation format (.ppt)

- Microsoft Word for Windows and Macintosh, version 6.0 (.doc)

- Plain text format (.txt)

The documents for each format are contained in the appropriately named subdirectory.

The CD-ROM is the copyright of BoardSource and is protected under federal copyright law. Any unlawful duplication of this CD-ROM is in violation of that copyright. Before customizing Microsoft Word or text documents, save a backup copy on your hard drive, and work from the copy on your hard drive.

## CONTENTS

Microsoft® PowerPoint® graphics presentation files

- *Presenting: Fundraising* presentation with talking points

Word files

- User's Guide for *Presenting: Fundraising*

Generic text files

- User's Guide for *Presenting: Fundraising*

The slides in the Microsoft® PowerPoint® graphics presentation format can be used as an on-screen presentation or printed as overhead transparency slides or handouts for board members. The CD-ROM also contains additional generic text files with the same information that appears on the slides and in the presentation notes and talking points. Use some or all of the sections depending on how they apply to your nonprofit.

We hope you enjoy the flexibility and customization capabilities of electronic text. If you have any questions regarding the files on this CD-ROM, please call BoardSource at 800-883-6262.

# Appendix 2. Board Fundraising Culture Assessment

As noted in Chapter 1, these questions can be distributed to board members as a prompt for discussion.

## BOARD FUNDRAISING CULTURE ASSESSMENT

1. Are prospective board members made aware of their fundraising responsibilities before they are elected to the board?

   ☐ yes       ☐ no       ☐ sort of / maybe / not certain

2. Are fundraising responsibilities and personal giving included in the board member expectation agreement?

   ☐ yes       ☐ no       ☐ sort of / maybe / not certain

3. Do all or almost all board members make a yearly personal "stretch" gift to the organization's annual fund?

   ☐ yes       ☐ no       ☐ sort of / maybe / not certain

4. Does the board chair personally solicit board members annually to ensure appropriate board giving? Does the board chair take time to personally cultivate and steward appropriate higher level prospects and donors?

   ☐ yes       ☐ no       ☐ sort of / maybe / not certain

5. Does the executive director take time to personally cultivate and steward appropriate higher level prospects and donors?

   ☐ yes       ☐ no       ☐ sort of / maybe / not certain

6. Does the board's fundraising committee organize the board's fundraising rather than actually doing the fundraising itself?

   ☐ yes       ☐ no       ☐ sort of / maybe / not certain

7. Is the organization's mission statement clear, concise, and compelling? Can all or almost all board members recite it?

   ☐ yes       ☐ no       ☐ sort of / maybe / not certain

8. Beyond just reciting the organization's mission statement, can at least 80 percent of board members convincingly articulate the case for support of the organization?

   ☐ yes ☐ no ☐ sort of / maybe / not certain

9. Does the director of development (or other staff person) identify appropriate cultivation and stewardship opportunities for board member participation?

   ☐ yes ☐ no ☐ sort of / maybe / not certain

10. Have the chief executive and director of development presented a clear fundraising strategy to the board and solicited board input?

    ☐ yes ☐ no ☐ sort of / maybe / not certain

11. Do the chief executive and board chair organize meeting agendas to give clear priority to fundraising?

    ☐ yes ☐ no ☐ sort of / maybe / not certain

12. Do the chief executive and board chair plan annually for board training opportunities in fundraising?

    ☐ yes ☐ no ☐ sort of / maybe / not certain

13. Do the chief executive, board chair, and director of development publicly acknowledge and recognize board members who are fulfilling their fundraising responsibilities?

    ☐ yes ☐ no ☐ sort of / maybe / not certain

Source: Adapted from materials used by Loring, Sternberg & Associates.

# Appendix 3. Fundraising Role-Playing Exercises

These exercises will help you as a board member develop confidence and enthusiasm for the fundraising process. They can be facilitated by the chief executive, the board chair, or an external party such as a consultant. The exercises should be done with the entire board, not just the fundraising or development committee.

These role plays are designed to give you a sense of the different aspects of the fundraising process: cultivation, solicitation, and stewardship. Remember that only solicitation is asking for a gift. A personal visit can have numerous outcomes, such as a return visit for more conversation, a request for a site visit, or an invitation for a prospect or donor to join a task force.

## GENERAL INSTRUCTIONS

- Read all of the material in this appendix, including the scenarios and the instructions for the facilitator, before you begin. Doing so will give you an overview of the exercises and will help you get a sense of what the exercises are trying to teach.

- Divide into groups of three. Each person in a group should select a role:

    #1: Team Member 1

    #2: Team Member 2

    #3: Prospective Donor

- Read through the entire scenario (provided later in this appendix) that the facilitator has given your group. Assume that there is a personal connection between the #2 and the #3 and therefore this will not be a "cold call."

- #3 should leave the room while #1 and #2 prepare their solicitation. #2 will be the one to ask for the gift. Use the following guidelines to help yourselves prepare.

## GUIDELINES FOR APPROACHING A PROSPECT

1. Start with small talk to establish warmth and rapport.

2. Introduce the subject

    - State purpose of your visit: "We are here to…"

    - Describe the major opportunity/need.

    - State what is needed to address the opportunity/need.

    - Explore the prospect's relationship to the opportunity/need with questions: What do you think are our biggest challenges? How do you feel about them? How might you address them?

- Summarize your understanding of the prospect's perspective and ask, "Is this correct?"

- After concurrence, ask, "Would you like to hear how our (program service, activities) will meet this need?" This leads into the presentation by creating interest and desire.

3. Get to the point

- Address the prospect by name.

- Explain your own involvement

  — If soliciting: "Let me tell you why I have made a gift..."

  — If cultivating: "Let me tell you why I feel so strongly about..."

  — If stewarding: "Let me share with you the outcomes from..."

  — If cultivating or soliciting, invite the prospect to join you.

4. Be prepared to explain

- The case/service of major emphasis

- Why the prospect would be interested

- The values exchange or benefit to the prospect

- The relationship between the prospect and your organization

5. Make the close (if soliciting)

- Ask your prospect, "Do you think our programs and plans will solve the problem(s)?"

- Prepare to handle objections and provide reassurances.

- State the benefits of meeting the need and ask the prospect to join or become a part of the organization and its campaign.

- Re-establish areas of agreement.

- Find areas of disagreement and convert them to agreement.

- Suggest something different, such as "Before you make your final decision, may we suggest...."

- Continue the process as long as rapport has been maintained and you have something new to add.

6. Things to remember

- Give reassurance regarding the project and its benefits.

- Plan what to say if you receive a "no." Often "no" is an invitation to offer further details or answer concerns. Fleeing from a "no" is costly and can prevent furthering potentially positive relationships.

- Plan what you will do if you find yourself in a position to negotiate a gift amount or another meeting date. You have decided to invest time in this prospect so make the most of it.

- Don't overstay your welcome. Keep within the time limits you promised when you made the appointment.

## INSTRUCTIONS FOR THE FACILITATOR

- Assign a different scenario to each group of three.

- Make certain that you give the #1 and #2 sufficient time to answer the questions necessary to approach the prospect (15-20 minutes).

- Ask the prospect (#3) to leave the room as the pair prepares. When #1 and #2 are ready, have them ask the prospect to join them. Give the group about 45 minutes to run through its scenario.

- Once all of the groups have completed the role-playing exercise, lead a debriefing period.

  — Ask each prospect to answer the following: Did the team listen well? What advice would you give them moving forward?

  — Ask each board and staff team if they would do things differently now that they have had a chance to practice.

  — Ask the entire group what they have learned. Listen for important feedback about the process and the experience.

## SCENARIO 1. TWO VOLUNTEERS — A CULTIVATION VISIT

#1. Board Member

- You have the responsibility of assisting in the fundraising activities of the organization.

- You serve on the development committee.

- You have a working knowledge of the programs and services of the organization and occasionally work closely with program delivery staff.

#2. Board Chair

- You are serving your second year in this position and have been on the board for five years.

- You are a successful professional and long-time community resident. You exert much influence and are active and well known in the community.

- You are an interested board member and are planning on giving $2,500 this year.

- Your income is about $100,000 and some of this is from investments.

- You are a large annual donor to a local nonprofit that is considered prestigious in the community.

- You personally know the prospect.

#3. Prospect

- You are a peer of the board chair because of your social and economic position in the community.

- You are president and owner of a business with estimated gross revenue of $30 million a year.

- You have approximately 150 employees.

- You have inquired about this organization, but other than the board chair you have only limited knowledge about its programs/services.

## Scenario 2. Staff and Board Team Solicitation

#1. Chief Executive

- You have the responsibility of managing the organization.

- You have a working knowledge of the programs and services of the organization.

- You have been on staff for three years.

- The organization has determined that this prospect is ready to be asked for an annual gift.

#2. Board Member

- You are serving your first year on the board, but have experience from other boards.

- You are retired and earn enough money from your investments to live comfortably.

- You know the prospect because he/she worked in your firm.

- You have a summer home in Florida.

- You are a widow(er) and have two grown children and three grandchildren.

- You are very passionate and wish you could give more than you do annually to many charities.

#3. Prospect

- You are involved in your community and serve on another nonprofit board.

- You are married and have two young children.

- You and your spouse earn $75,000 a year.

- As a baby boomer, you need to feel as though every dollar you contribute goes to programming.

- Planning for your children's future is a big priority for you.

## SCENARIO 3 — EXPLORING OPTIONS THROUGH STEWARDSHIP

#1. Chief Executive

- You have the responsibility of managing the organization.

- You have a working knowledge of the programs and services of the organization.

- You have been on staff for three years.

- The organization has determined that this prospect needs to be visited to receive a thank you in person and to discuss if planned giving is something worth exploring moving forward.

#2. Board Member

- You are an annual donor and have made a significant planned gift.

- You are active on the board and enjoy speaking publicly about the organization.

- You know the prospect from a service club/organization.

#3. Prospect

- You are the president of a major company and planning for retirement in the next two years.

- Currently you earn over $500,000 plus incentives and hold over $10 million in stock options.

- You are married and have no children.

- Your spouse is extremely involved in a number of civic organizations to which you both contribute.

- You are a donor to the organization and are active as a volunteer.

# Appendix 4. Sample Board Member Letter of Agreement

As a board member of XYZ Organization, I am fully committed to the mission and have pledged to help carry it out. I understand that my duties and responsibilities include the following:

1. I will be fiscally responsible, with other board members, for this organization. I will know what our budget is and take an active part in reviewing, approving, and monitoring the budget.

2. I know my legal responsibilities for this organization as a member of the board and will take an active part in establishing and overseeing the organization's policies and programs.

3. I will act in accordance with the bylaws and operating principles outlined in the manual and understand that I am morally responsible, as a member of the board, for the health and well-being of this organization.

4. I will give what is for me a personally sacrificial annual financial donation.

5. I will actively participate in fundraising in whatever ways are best suited for me and agreed on with those in charge of the organization's fundraising. These may include individual solicitations, undertaking special events, writing mail appeals, and the like. I am making a good-faith agreement to do my best and to help raise as much money as I can.

6. I will actively promote XYZ in the community and will encourage and support its staff.

7. I will prepare for and attend all board meetings, be available for phone consultation, and serve on at least one committee as needed.

8. If I am not able to meet my obligations as a board member, I will offer my resignation.

9. In signing this document, I understand that no quotas are being set and that no rigid standards of measurement and achievement are being formed and trust that all board members will carry out the above agreements to the best of our ability.

Board Member _____        _____
                        *Signature*                                    *Date*

Board Chair _____        _____
                        *Signature*                                    *Date*

Source: *The Board Building Cycle: Nine Steps to Finding, Recruiting, and Engaging Nonprofit Board Members, Second Edition* by Berit M. Lakey (BoardSource, 2007)

# *Appendix 5. The BoardSource Fundraising Checklist*

## FUNDRAISING RESPONSIBILITIES AND OPPORTUNITIES FOR NONPROFIT BOARD MEMBERS

This inventory offers several benefits. First, it expands the notion of fundraising to include many activities other than asking for donations. It also solicits concrete information from individual board members about which tasks they are willing to complete. Finally, it provides a snapshot of the board's self-confidence and capacity, allowing the staff to provide customized support materials.

---

**How many are YOU willing to consider and undertake?**

Mark each:   Y = yes   N = no   M = maybe (no more than 10 maybes)

**Be honest. Be realistic. Be willing to try something new.**

---

### Level One: Planning and Building

_____ 1. **Commit** to the organization's vision and mission. Be willing to learn more about how to give and get contributed resources.

_____ 2. **Provide** informed input into a market-oriented planning process (help decide which goals deserve priority given organizational capabilities, resources, depth of volunteer commitment, and implementation strategies).

_____ 3. **Aid** in the creation of the fund development plan. Understand the plan's implication. Be willing to help execute it. If you cannot, state why this is and be willing to work toward consensus on some revisions.

_____ 4. **Assist** in drafting the fundraising case statement — a comprehensive justification for charitable support — and be able to explain this rationale persuasively.

_____ 5. **Decide** realistic budget allocations for the organization's fundraising program. (Be patient about how fast new income will be received, but ask questions, offer suggestions, and operate by agreed-upon procedures and assignments.)

_____ 6. **Review, critique, and monitor** the action strategy — a policy and procedure outline of how and when the program is to be implemented. (This could be about types of fundraising on which to concentrate; methods of approach; ways to identify target markets; or how gifts are to be sought, allocated, reported, acknowledged, and then leveraged for more along with specific benchmarks to measure outcomes.)

_____ 7. **Understand** the organization's financial situation and probable future funding position. Resist quick fixes and short-range decisions. Probe until you become convinced money is wisely used and staff is accountable.

_____ 8. **Evaluate** progress by asking friendly but searching questions. (Are we doing what we agreed to do? If not, why not? Are we getting improved results as time goes on? What specifically? If not, why not? What reasonable changes might be explored? What do we require that is not available currently? Expertise? Staff time? Volunteers? Commitment level?)

_____ 9. **Join and get active** on at least one board committee and be alert for how its work can strengthen current fundraising endeavors. (Almost every aspect of the operation has some impact on development, directly or indirectly.)

_____ 10. **Approve** the creation or revision of a board member statement of responsibilities that includes clearly defined expectations for their personal giving and involvement in fundraising.

---

## Level Two: Friend Raising

_____ 11. **Provide** the names and addresses of donor prospects for the development mailing list. Share pertinent information about your contacts: individual preferences, interest level, any misgivings about the cause, and their inclination to donate money.

_____ 12. **Research** phone numbers or secure exact addresses for campaign mailings.

_____ 13. **Attend** training workshop(s) to discover how better to carry out your role and to augment the overall development process.

_____ 14. **Prepare** useful and informative training materials for board members and other volunteers about how to raise funds.

_____ 15. **Recruit** volunteers and prospective helpers and suggest ways to interest and to involve persons with whom you or your friends are acquainted.

_____ 16. **Advocate** for the organization or case and serve as an enthusiastic community relations representative. (Understand the organization's mission and programs and be prepared to answer common questions. Prompt others in the community to begin participating in the work of the organization.)

_____ 17. **Acquire** mailing lists from a variety of sources in the community to augment the organization's database.

_____ 18. **Facilitate** introductions and access to individuals or groups where you have credibility and influence. Nurture prospects and donors on a regular basis.

_____ 19. **Distribute** (hand deliver) invitations or promotional material to targeted markets: individuals, business, churches, temples, community groups, or clubs.

_____ 20. **Cultivate** more varied media contacts for wider publicity and promotion. Link your organization with regional councils, societies, or associations. Seek out wider sponsorship for events, programs, or educational sessions.

_____ 21. **Join** the speakers bureau or agree to be a spokesperson for your organization at some specific occasion or event.

_____ 22. **Spearhead** the formation of a business and professional advisory group and encourage one of your own professional advisors (such as a CPA or an attorney) to become involved.

_____ 23. **Find and relate** one or more human-interest stories to illustrate why gifts are needed and how they are used to provide, enhance, or expand your organization's outreach and impact.

_____ 24. **Brainstorm** innovative ways to thank and to recognize donors. For instance, arrange a special "thank-a-thon" in which board members phone donors to express gratitude for their contributions, with no solicitation included in the conversation.

_____ 25. **Research** individual prospects, foundations, and corporate funding sources through public information sources. Locate promotional partners or establish a join venture. Summarize your findings for staff or committee use.

_____ 26. **Write** a personal testimonial or letter of support for public use or agree to be quoted as to why you support the organization.

_____ 27. **Hand-deliver** thank-yous, acknowledgments, or special awards to volunteers, contributors, or support groups.

_____ 28. **Participate** in an evaluation session, during which you help campaign leaders gather the information they need about giving patterns and capacity of identified prospects.

_____ 29. **Assist** in fundraising special events, such as auctions, fairs, bazaars, open houses, tours, or tournaments. Enlist others to help in ways that they perceive are useful and fun, so they will want to do it again. Welcome newcomers; circulate and mingle to spread a friendly spirit, learn names, and discover common interests.

_____ 30. **Sell** products, tickets, or premiums where proceeds directly benefit your organization.

_____ 31. **Visit** a community leader to explain needs to be met and accomplishments of the organization. Initiate follow-up visits to sustain and increase interest.

_____32. **Host** — in your home or at a restaurant — a small group volunteers or donor prospects to better acquaint them with the value of your organization's priorities: educational programs, advancement of a cause, or effective human-services delivery.

_____33. **Establish** a planned giving program by finding ways to underline the importance of a remember-us-in-your-will emphasis.

---

### Level Three: Solicitation

_____34. **Contact** local businesses and vendor suppliers to seek an in-kind donation, such as supplies, equipment, technical assistance, or personnel (interns, release time, loaned executives, etc.).

_____35. **Personalize** the annual direct-mail program or other endorsed campaign by using at least two of the following techniques:

- Hand address envelopes for use with top donors.
- Add a personal P.S. or thank you on the prepared acknowledgment.
- Compose and send your note of appreciation for a gift.
- Phone to thank some of those who responded.

_____36. **Increase** your donation each year to help reach the goal and assist in setting the place for others, so that you will become a credible solicitor.

_____37. **Request** a pledge or a contribution from designated prospects or lapsed donors.

_____38. **Solicit** a cash contribution from a service club, civic group, or church or temple, or request a gift for a particular promotion or publication.

_____39. **Accept** a leadership role to recognize solicitation teams or a specific campaign.

_____40. **Ask** selected individuals for a specific gift or a multiyear pledge. Visit them personally, accompanied by a staff member or another volunteer.

# Suggested Resources

BoardSource. *Speaking of Money: A Guide to Fundraising for Nonprofit Board Members.* Washington, DC: BoardSource 1996. Former ABC News journalist Hugh Downs walks viewers through a series of candid interviews in which real board members explain why fundraising is an essential board responsibility, how board members work in partnership with staff, and how to ask for a gift. Equally suitable for use at board orientation sessions, development committee meetings, or board retreats, *Speaking of Money* is a thoughtful, inspiring, and humorous look at a critical board responsibility.

Fredricks, Laura. *The Ask: How to Ask Anyone for Any Amount for Any Purpose.* San Francisco, CA: Jossey-Bass, 2006. *The Ask* is a complete resource for teaching anyone — experienced in fundraising or not — how to ask individuals, in person, for a contribution to a local nonprofit or a special event or community project, an enhanced annual gift, a major or planned gift, or a challenging capital campaign gift. Written by fundraising expert Laura Fredricks, *The Ask* shows what it takes to prepare yourself and others to make an effective ask and includes over 100 sample dialogues you can use and adapt. Step by step, the book reveals how to listen, what to say, and how to follow up on each and every ask until you receive a solid and definitive answer.

Grace, Kay Sprinkel. *Beyond Fundraising: New Strategies for Nonprofit Innovation and Investment, 2nd Edition.* New York, NY: John Wiley & Sons, 2005. In this revised and updated Second Edition, fundraising expert Kay Sprinkel Grace presents her internationally field-tested core beliefs, principles, and strategies for developing long-term relationships with donor-investors and volunteers. Share in the wisdom and experience that have helped countless nonprofit organizations grow their base of support and go beyond fundraising into true donor and fund development.

Greenfield, James M. *Fundraising Responsibilities of Nonprofit Boards.* Washington, DC: BoardSource, 2004. Discover why fundraising is important and why board members should be involved. Included in *Fundraising Responsibilities of Nonprofit Boards* are practical suggestions for board members in direction, planning, and oversight of fundraising. Help your board succeed in the three phases of fundraising — cultivation, solicitation, and stewardship.

Hopkins, Bruce R. *The Law of Fundraising, 3rd Edition.* New York, NY: John Wiley & Sons, 2008. Completely updated and expanded, this Third Edition of *The Law of Fundraising* is the only book to tackle the increasingly complex maze of federal and state fundraising regulations. Written by one of the country's few legal experts on fundraising laws pertaining to tax-exempt organizations, this comprehensive reference details federal and state laws with an emphasis on administrative, tax, and constitutional law. Exploring compliance issues, prospective laws, and regulatory trends, this authoritative resource also provides you with summaries of each state's Charitable Contribution Solicitation Act, the most important regulation impacting fundraising practice and professionals within each state.

Mutz, John, and Katherine Murray. *Fundraising for Dummies, 2nd Edition*. New York, NY: John Wiley & Sons, 2005. Whether you're a small outfit or a big organization, you're competing for donors' dollars and time. This hands-on, vital guide shows you how to take full advantage of the strategies and resources available and advises you how to promote your cause, research potential donors, organize events, write winning grant proposals, and utilize the latest technology.

Seiler, Timothy L. *Developing Your Case for Support*. Hoboken NJ: John Wiley & Sons, 2001. A carefully crafted case for support is the cornerstone of successful fundraising. Tim Seiler, a leader in the fundraising field, explains the process a nonprofit should go through to present a coherent statement of the reasons why it is worthy of support. Numerous worksheets and examples guide an organization in drafting a winning case statement.

Tempel, Eugene R. *Development Committee*. Washington, DC: BoardSource, 2004. *Development Committee* brings with it a necessary clarity in defining what the roles and responsibilities of a development committee are and how to work together with board and staff members to make them effective. This book teaches board members how to take a more hands-on position in board leadership as they participate in fundraising for the organization — straying from the normal oversight and policy-making role of the board. Discover how to use different people in a variety of ways in order to build relationships with donors and members of the community.

# About the Author

Dave Sternberg has been a fundraising professional for 17 years. His career began after earning his BA degree from the Ohio State University. He served as the chief development officer for a small Greek letter education foundation, as the assistant director of annual giving at Butler University and as the acting director of development for a state chapter of the Prevention of Child Abuse.

In 1996, Dave founded Loring, Sternberg and Associates based in Indianapolis, Ind. Dave's fundraising counsel to educational foundations, social service organizations, higher education, membership organizations, children's groups, and museums includes strategic planning, development audits, ongoing fund development planning, planning studies and campaign direction, and most frequently board fundraising training.

Dave is also a member of the faculty of the Fund Raising School at the Center on Philanthropy at Indiana University where he teaches both nationally and internationally.

Dave is active in the Association of Fundraising Professionals Indiana Chapter serving two terms as the vice president of programs (1999, 2000) and as the chapter president 2001. In addition, he served two years as the chair of Indiana Fund Raising Day in 1997 and 1998.

In July of 2004, Dave added the role of associate director of public service for the Center on Philanthropy at Indiana University, the Fund Raising School as part of his portfolio.